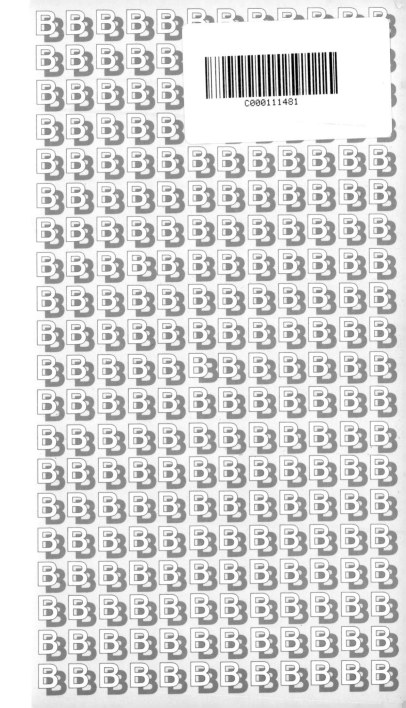

C000111481

英語で日本料理
100 Recipes from Japanese Cooking

辻調理師専門学校
畑耕一郎 | 近藤一樹

はじめに

　近頃は、海外にも日本料理店が増えてきて、以前に比べ日本食も知られるようになりましたが、高価なこともあり、まだまだ一般の人が楽しむまでには程遠いようです。

　そこで、日本料理がもっと身近なものとなることを願って、外国人と交流のある人、たとえば海外でのホームスティを計画している学生さん、単身赴任で海外出張をする会社員の方、あるいは自宅に外国人を招く機会の多い方たちのために、和英両文で日本料理を楽しみながら作り、料理と英語の能力を高めようという欲張りなクックブックが本書です。

　日常、日本の家庭の食卓にのぼる馴染み深い料理を中心に、ごく簡単なレシピから、いくらか上級のプロのにおいがするものまで、おいしくてなつかしい料理を100品収録しました。

　日頃まったく料理をしない男性でも失敗なくできるようにわかりやすく、そしてすこし手慣れた人にはプロの味に挑戦できるよう、手順も丁寧に解説しています。

　料理をおいしく作るのは、とても簡単なことです。それは始める前に必要な材料と道具をそろえること、そして、本書をよく読んで指導の通りに決して手抜きをしないこと、それだけでいいのです。

　何度も挑戦して、あなたの自慢料理をひとつずつ増やしお客さんをもてなしてください。料理の腕前も英語の腕前も楽しみながら上達していくことは間違いありません。

　大切なのは、まず始めること、そして続けることです。

畑　耕一郎
大阪あべの辻調理師専門学校—日本料理主任教授

PREFACE

Japanese restaurants overseas are growing apace, and Japanese food is becoming ever more popular. However, Japanese cuisine can be a costly pleasure and remains for most only an occasional one.

With the hope of making Japanese cooking more accessible, we have created this cookbook for people interested in both cooking Japanese food and bettering their English—students planning a home stay abroad, business people living alone overseas, or anyone who enjoys inviting foreign friends to their homes.

For the most part, our 100 recipes are examples of everyday Japanese cooking. They include both extremely simple recipes and a few that an experienced chef would be proud of.

Even for those with no previous cooking experience, the directions are easy to follow. At the same time, though, we've written with enough detail to enable skilled cooks to aim at professional results.

Remember, good cooking is the product of a few simple habits. Have all your ingredients and cooking tools ready in advance. Read through the entire recipe before beginning. Then follow the recipe exactly, taking care not to skip any steps.

Try out the recipes one by one, make them your own, and invite over some friends. Your cooking and English skills will improve together, while having a great time. So, let's get started!

Hata Koichiro
Head of the Japanese cookery department
Ecole Technique Hôtelière Tsuji in Abeno, Osaka

本書の決まり・NOTES

● 材料は、特に表示のない場合は、すべて4人分です。

● エネルギー(kcal)の数値は、ことわりのない場合以外は、1人分(1個分)です。

● 計量の単位は、大さじ1が15cc、小さじ1が5ccで、すりきりで計ります。

● 計量カップ1は、日本では200cc、アメリカでは240ccと、かなり違います。本書では、和文に関しては出来るだけカップ表示をやめ、ccを使いましたが、英文には、アメリカで料理をする時のことを考えて、アメリカンカップ(U.S. cup)の単位を使っています。240頁の度量衡早見表を参照してください。

● 作り方をひと通り読んで、必要な材料や道具をそろえ、手順がスムーズにいくようにして始めてください。

● Unless noted, all recipes are for four servings.

● Unless noted, the kcal figure gives the number of calories contained in one serving.

● One tablespoon is the equivalent of 15cc, and one teaspoon is 5 cc, both measured flat.

● Japanese and U.S. measurements differ significantly. In Japan, one cup equals 200cc; in the United States, 240cc. In this book, the metric measure is used in Japanese recipes when possible. For the convenience of readers in America, however, "cup" is used in the English-language recipes. See the table of measurements on page 240.

● For smooth cooking, be sure to read through the recipe in advance and have all your ingredients and cooking tools close at hand.

汁 物 | SOUPS

RICE

すし | SUSHI

VINEGARED and DRESSED DISHES

造り

SASHIMI DISHES

鍋物 **ONE-POT DISHES**

焼き物 GRILLED and PAN-FRIED DISHES

煮物 | SIMMERED DISHES

揚げ物 | # DEEP-FRIED DISHES

❶

蒸し物 | STEAMED DISHES

麺 | NOODLES

お菓子 | SWEETS

目 次 • CONTENTS

すし • SUSHI

酢の物・あえ物 • VINEGARED and DRESSED DISHES

焼き物 • GRILLED and PAN-FRIED DISHES

煮物 • SIMMERED DISHES

揚げ物 • DEEP-FRIED DISHES

蒸し物 • STEAMED DISHES

麺 • NOODLES

お菓子 • SWEETS

だし

◆材 料 (1000 ccのだし)

水　1000 cc
昆布　10 cm (20 g)
削り節 (花がつお)
　1つかみ (20〜30 g)

◆作り方

1　昆布はかたく絞ったぬれ布巾で汚れをふき取る。→❶

2　鍋に分量の水と昆布を入れ、中火にかけ、沸騰寸前に昆布を取り出す。→❷

3　少量の水 (50cc) を注ぎ、沸騰をおさえる。→❸

4　削り節を加え、沸騰したら火をとめる。→❹

5　アクを取る。→❺

6　削り節が沈んだら、布巾でこす。→❻

❶

❷

❸

Dashi (Basic Stock)

◆ DIRECTIONS

1   Wipe *konbu* kelp lightly with a well-wrung damp cloth to clean. →❶

2   Place water and *konbu* in a soup pot over medium heat. Remove *konbu* just before water reaches a boil. →❷

3   Add 1²⁄₃ oz water to keep from boiling. →❸

4   Add bonito flakes. When the water boils, remove from heat at once. →❹

5   Skim the surface to remove foam. →❺

6   When bonito flakes sink to the bottom, strain through a cheesecloth-lined sieve. →❻

◆ INGREDIENTS
 (Makes 4 U.S. cups)

4 U.S. cups water
4-inch (²⁄₃ oz) *konbu* kelp
I handful (²⁄₃–I oz) dried bonito flakes

❹

❺

❻

豆腐とわかめのみそ汁

1人分 50 kcal

◆材　料(4人分)

絹ごし豆腐　½丁 (150 g)

わかめ (乾燥)　5 g

青ねぎ　1本

汁
- だし　600 cc
- 赤みそ　60 g

粉ざんしょう　少々

◆作り方

1　豆腐は、1cm角のさいの目に切る。

2　わかめは水につけてもどし、2cm幅に切る。

3　青ねぎは小口切りにし、水にさらして、水けをきる(さらしねぎ)。

4　だしを火にかけ、一煮立ちしたら、だしで柔らかくのばしたみそを入れ、味を見る*。→❶

5　豆腐とわかめを加え、仕上げにさらしねぎを入れて火をとめる。

6　椀によそい、好みで粉ざんしょうをふる。

＊みそは種類によって味はさまざま。味見をして、入れる量はかげんすること。

メ　モ
- みそはじかに入れないで溶きのばすこと。
- みそを入れたらグラグラ煮立てないこと。

❶

Tofu and *Wakame* Seaweed Miso Soup

Tōfu to Wakame no Miso-shiru

50 kcal per serving

◆ DIRECTIONS

1 Cut tofu into 3/8-inch cubes.

2 Soak *wakame* seaweed in cold water, and cut into 3/4-inch strips.

3 Chop scallion finely, rinse in cold water and drain ("rinsed scallions").

4 Place *dashi* in a soup pot, bring to a boil. Soften miso by adding a small amount of *dashi*, add to pot, and taste.*
→❶

5 Add tofu and *wakame* and boil briefly. Add scallion, and immediately turn off heat.

6 Transfer to soup bowls and sprinkle with *sansho* pepper.

＊The flavor and saltiness of miso differs from type to type. Taste to adjust the seasoning.

NOTES
• Soften miso with some stock before adding to the stock. Do not add miso directly.
• Boil as briefly as possible after adding miso.

◆ INGREDIENTS (4 servings)

1/2 cake (5 1/4 oz) "silken" tofu
1/6 oz dried *wakame* seaweed
1 scallion
Soup
⎡ 2 1/2 U.S. cups *dashi*
⎣ 2 oz red miso
ground *sansho* pepper

かきたま汁

1人分 60 kcal

◆材　料 (4人分)

卵　2個

三つ葉　½束 (25 g)

汁
- だし　600 cc
- 塩　小さじ¾
- 薄口しょうゆ　小さじ2
- 水溶き片栗粉*
  - 片栗粉　大さじ2
  - 水　大さじ2

しょうがの絞り汁　小さじ1

＊水溶き片栗粉：片栗粉を
同量の水で溶いたもの

◆作り方

1　卵は溶きほぐす。三つ葉は2cm長さに切る。

2　鍋にだし、塩、薄口しょうゆを入れて軽く沸騰させる。

3　水溶き片栗粉を少しずつ加え、とろみをつける。

4　卵を渦巻きを描くように流し入れ、軽くかき混ぜる。

5　三つ葉としょうがの絞り汁を加え、火をとめる。

Beaten Egg Soup

Kakitama-jiru

60 kcal per serving

◆ DIRECTIONS

1 Beat eggs lightly. Cut *mitsuba* into ³/₄-inch lengths.

2 Place *dashi*, salt, and light soy sauce in a soup pot, and bring to a boil.

3 Add starch-water mixture gradually to thicken.

4 Swirl in beaten egg, rotating the pot. Stir lightly.

5 Add *mitsuba* and ginger juice, and turn off heat.

◆ INGREDIENTS (4 servings)

2 eggs
¹/₂ bunch (⁷/₈ oz) *mitsuba* (trefoil)
Soup
  ⎰ 2¹/₂ U.S. cups *dashi*
  ⎱ ³/₄ tsp salt
  ⎰ 2 tsp light soy sauce
  ⎱ starch-water mixture*
      ⎰ 2 Tbsp cornstarch
      ⎱ 2 Tbsp water
1 tsp fresh ginger juice

*Starch-water mixture: Dissolve starch with an equal portion of water.

豚汁

1人分 200 kcal

◆材 料 (4人分)

豚ロース肉 (薄切り) 150 g
ごぼう 1 本 (70 g)
さつま芋 50 g
にんじん 50 g
大根 70 g
こんにゃく 50 g
青ねぎ 2 本
汁
[だし 800 cc
[赤みそ 80 g
一味唐がらし 少々

◆作り方

1 豚肉は一口大に切る。

2 ごぼうはよく洗い、細い方から削る
ように粗い笹がきにする。すぐに水に
さらして、水けをきる。→❶

3 さつま芋、にんじん、大根は3mm厚さの
短冊切りにする。

4 こんにゃくは同じ大きさの短冊切りに
して熱湯でさっとゆでる。

5 青ねぎは斜め切りにする。

6 鍋にだしを入れ、青ねぎ以外の材料を
加えて火にかけ、アクを取りながら
柔らかくなるまで煮る。

7 みそを溶き入れて軽く煮込み、仕上げ
に青ねぎを加える。

8 椀によそい、一味唐がらしをふる。

❶

Miso Soup with Pork and Vegetables
Ton-jiru

200 kcal per serving

◆ DIRECTIONS

1 Cut pork into bite-sized pieces.

2 Wash and scrub burdock thoroughly, and shave from the skinnier end. Immediately soak in water, and drain. →❶

3 Cut sweet potato, carrot, *daikon* radish and *konnyaku* into about 1½ × ⅜-inch rectangular pieces, about ⅛-inch thick.

4 Blanch *konnyaku* in boiling water.

5 Sliver scallions diagonally.

6 Place *dashi* and all ingredients except scallions in a soup pot, and boil until tender, skimming occasionally.

7 Soften miso with some soup, add to the pot, and simmer lightly. Add scallions and turn off heat.

8 Transfer to soup bowls and sprinkle with chili pepper flakes.

◆ INGREDIENTS (4 servings)

5¼ oz thinly sliced pork loin
1 (2½ oz) burdock root
1¾ oz sweet potato
1¾ oz carrot
2½ oz *daikon* radish
1¾ oz *konnyaku* (devil's tongue jelly)
2 scallions
Soup
⎰ 3⅓ U.S. cups *dashi*
⎱ 2⅘ oz red miso
chili pepper flakes

はまぐりのうしお汁

1人分　30 kcal

◆材料(4人分)

はまぐり　8個 (450 g)
塩　適量
えのきだけ　½パック (50 g)
わかめ (乾燥)　3 g
汁
[水　800 cc
　昆布　5 cm
　酒　小さじ1
　薄口しょうゆ　小さじ1
　塩　少々]
しょうがのせん切り*
　1かけ (20 g)

*皮をむき、薄切りにし、
少しずつずらして置いて
端から細切りにする。

◆作り方

1　はまぐりは塩水 (水200ccに塩小さじ
1の割合) につけて、砂を吐かせる。
殻と殻をこすりつけて、よく洗う。→❶❷

2　えのきだけは根元を切り落とし、
小分けにする。

3　わかめは水でもどし、4cm幅に切る。

4　鍋に水、昆布、はまぐりを入れて火に
かける。沸騰寸前に昆布を取り出し、
アクを取る。はまぐりの口が開いたら貝を
取り出し、身は殻からはずしておく。

5　汁を布巾でこし、砂を取り除く。
再び火にかけ、酒、薄口しょうゆ、塩で
味を調える。

6　えのきだけとわかめを加えてさっと
火を通す。

7　椀に殻1個と身2個を入れ、えのきだけ、
わかめを盛って汁を注ぎ、しょうがの
せん切りをのせる。

メモ
•ひな祭りや祝いごとの際によく作られる汁物。
•うしお汁とは、だしを使わずに、魚介類の味を
生かした吸い物。

❶　❷

Clam Soup

Hamaguri no Ushio-jiru

30 kcal per serving

◆ DIRECTIONS

1 Soak clams in salted water (1 tsp salt to 6²/₃ oz water) to let them expel sand. Wash well, rubbing shells against each other. →❶❷

2 Cut away root cluster of the *enoki* mushrooms, and separate into smaller pieces.

3 Soak *wakame* in cold water, and cut into 1¹/₂-inch strips.

4 Place water, *konbu*, and clams in a soup pot and heat. Remove *konbu* just before boiling and skim foam. Remove clams when open, take the meat from the shells.

5 Strain the broth to discard sand. Reheat the strained broth, and season with *saké*, light soy sauce, and salt.

6 Add *enoki* mushrooms and *wakame*, and heat briefly.

7 In each bowl, place meat of two clams in one shell, add *enoki* and *wakame*. Fill bowls with hot broth, and top with slivered ginger.

NOTES
• This soup is often cooked for celebrations such as Doll Festival.
• *Ushio-jiru* is a type of clear soup which is made without dashi stock to bring out the seafood flavor of the main ingredients.

◆ INGREDIENTS (4 servings)

8 (1 lb) live hard-shell clams
salt
¹/₂ pack (1³/₄ oz) *enoki* mushrooms
¹/₈ oz dried *wakame* seaweed

Broth
- 3¹/₃ U.S. cups water
- 2-inch square *konbu* kelp
- 1 tsp *saké*
- 1 tsp light soy sauce
- pinch salt

²/₃ oz fresh ginger, finely slivered*

*Peel, slice thinly, stack the slabs with each edge overlapping slightly, and cut into fine julienne strips.

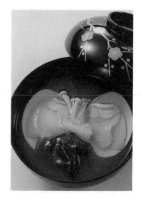

貝柱の沢煮わん

1人分 40 kcal

◆材　料(4人分)

帆立て貝の貝柱 (生)
　2個(100 g)
にんじん　30 g
生しいたけ　4枚
絹さや　8枚
汁
　┌ だし　600 cc
　│ 酒　大さじ1
　│ 塩　小さじ⅔
　└ 薄口しょうゆ　小さじ1
白こしょう　少々

◆作り方

1　貝柱は細切りにする。

2　にんじんは皮をむいてせん切り、
しいたけは軸をとって薄切り、絹さやは
筋をとって細切りにする。

3　だしににんじん、しいたけを入れて
火にかける。柔らかくなったら弱火にし、
アクを取り除き、酒、塩、薄口しょうゆで
味を調える。

4　貝柱と絹さやを加えて、一煮立ちさせ、
火をとめる。

5　椀によそい、白こしょうをふる。

メ モ
•沢(さわ)とは多くのという意味。

Scallop and Vegetable Soup, *Sawa*-style

Kaibashira no Sawani-wan

40 kcal per serving

◆ DIRECTIONS

1 Cut scallops into thin strips.

2 Peel carrot, string snow peas, and cut both into fine slivers. Slice mushroom caps thinly.

3 Place *dashi*, carrot, and *shiitake* mushrooms in a soup pot and heat. When vegetables are tender, lower heat and skim. Add *saké*, salt, and light soy sauce to season.

4 Add scallops and snow peas and bring to a boil, then remove from heat.

5 Transfer to soup bowls, and sprinkle with white pepper.

NOTE
• *Sawa* is a word meaning "many."

◆ INGREDIENTS (4 servings)

2 (3 1/2 oz) shucked scallops
1 oz carrot
4 fresh *shiitake* mushrooms
8 snow peas
Soup
   2 1/2 U.S. cups *dashi*
   1 Tbsp *saké*
   2/3 tsp salt
   1 tsp light soy sauce
white pepper

えびだんごのすまし汁

1人分 60 kcal

◆材 料(4人分)

えび (殻つき、無頭)
　12尾 (300 g)
塩　少々
片栗粉　大さじ1
しめじ　½パック (70 g)
ほうれん草　½束 (100 g)
汁
　┌ だし　600 cc
　│ 酒　小さじ½
　│ 塩　小さじ⅔
　└ 薄口しょうゆ　小さじ1
木の芽　8枚

◆作り方

1　えびは殻と背わた*を取り、包丁で
たたき、塩と片栗粉を入れてさらに
細かく刻む。4等分にして楕円形に丸め、
熱湯で7分ゆでる。

2　しめじは石づきを取って小分けにし、
熱湯でゆでる。

3　ほうれん草は塩ゆでし、水にさらして、
水けを絞り、4cm長さに切る。

4　鍋にだしと調味料を入れて一煮立ち
させ、味見をする。

5　椀に1のえびだんご、しめじ、
ほうれん草を盛り、熱い汁を注いで、
木の芽をのせる。

*背わたの取り方: 透き通って見える黒い筋が
背わた。背を丸めて頭から2〜3節目の殻と
殻の間に竹串を刺し込み、背わたをすくい、
引き抜く。

Clear Soup with Shrimp Balls

Ebi-dango no Sumashi-jiru

60 kcal per serving

◆ DIRECTIONS

1   Shell and devein shrimp* and chop finely, adding salt and cornstarch. Divide into 4 portions, form each into a ball, and cook 7 minutes in boiling water.

2   Cut away root clusters of the *shimeji* mushrooms, separate them slightly, and parboil.

3   Parboil spinach in lightly salted water, rinse in cold water, and squeeze out excess water. Then cut into 1½-inch lengths.

4   Place *dashi* and seasonings in a soup pot, bring to a boil, and taste.

5   Place a shrimp ball, mushrooms and spinach in each bowl. Add hot broth, and top with *kinome* sprigs.

*To devein shrimp: Expose the black stringy vein by gently bending the shrimp. Catch the vein by inserting a toothpick between the 2nd and 3rd shell segments, and pull it out.

◆ INGREDIENTS (4 servings)

12 (10½ oz) shrimp in shells without heads
dash salt
1 Tbsp cornstarch
½ pack (2½ oz) *shimeji* mushrooms
½ bunch (3½ oz) spinach
Broth
  ⎡ 2½ U.S. cups *dashi*
  ⎮ ½ tsp *saké*
  ⎮ ⅔ tsp salt
  ⎣ 1 tsp light soy sauce
8 *kinome* (prickly ash) sprigs

けんちん汁

1人分 230 kcal

◆材　料(4人分)

木綿豆腐　½丁 (150 g)
豚ロース肉 (薄切り)　150 g
生しいたけ　4枚
にんじん　50 g
たけのこ (水煮)　50 g
こんにゃく　50 g
三つ葉　1束 (50 g)
サラダ油　大さじ2
汁
　だし　600 cc
　塩　小さじ1
　薄口しょうゆ　小さじ2
水溶き片栗粉
　片栗粉　大さじ2
　水　大さじ2
しょうがの絞り汁　小さじ1
七味唐がらし　少々

◆作り方

1　豆腐は手で粗くつぶす。

2　豚肉は一口大に切る。しいたけは軸を取り、薄切りにする。にんじん、たけのこは4cm長さの細切りにする。こんにゃくは短冊切りにする。三つ葉は3cm長さに切る。

3　鍋に油少量を熱し、豚肉、こんにゃく、豆腐をさっといため、続いてにんじん、たけのこ、しいたけを加えていためる。

4　だし、塩、薄口しょうゆを加え、味を調え、三つ葉を加える。

5　水溶き片栗粉を流し入れてとろみをつけ、しょうがの絞り汁を加える。

6　椀によそい、好みで七味唐がらしをふる。

Tofu, Pork, and Vegetable Soup, *Kenchin*-style

Kenchin-jiru

230 kcal per serving

◆ DIRECTIONS

1   Crumble tofu coarsely by hand.

2   Cut pork into bite-sized pieces.
Slice *shiitake* mushroom caps, carrot,
and bamboo shoots into 1½-inch strips.
Slice *konnyaku* into thin rectangular
slabs. Cut *mitsuba* into 1-inch lengths.

3   Heat oil in a soup pot, and cook
pork, *konnyaku*, and tofu quickly.
Add carrot, bamboo shoots, and *shiitake*,
and stir-fry.

4   Add *dashi*, salt, and light soy sauce to
season. Add *mitsuba*.

5   Thicken soup with the starch-water
mixture, and add ginger juice.

6   Transfer to soup bowls, and sprinkle
with seven-spice pepper.

◆ INGREDIENTS (4 servings)

½ cake (5¼ oz)
   "cotton" tofu
5¼ oz thinly sliced
   pork loin
4 fresh *shiitake* mushrooms
1¾ oz carrot
1¾ oz boiled bamboo
   shoots
1¾ oz *konnyaku*
   (devil's tongue jelly)
1 bunch (1¾ oz) *mitsuba*
   (trefoil)
2 Tbsp vegetable oil
Soup
  ⎡ 2½ U.S. cups *dashi*
  ⎨ 1 tsp salt
  ⎣ 2 tsp light soy sauce
starch-water mixture
  ⎡ 2 Tbsp cornstarch
  ⎣ 2 Tbsp water
1 tsp fresh ginger juice
seven-spice pepper

お雑煮

1人分 260 kcal

◆材 料 (4人分)

鶏胸肉　120 g
大根　100 g
にんじん　50 g
生しいたけ　4枚
里芋　2個 (100 g)
三つ葉　1束 (50 g)
もち　4個
汁
  ┌ だし　600 cc
  └ 白みそ　120 g
ゆずの皮 (細切り)　少々

◆作り方

1　鶏肉は5mm厚さに切り、熱湯でゆでて火を通す。

2　大根は5mm厚さ、にんじんは2mm厚さのいちょう切りにする。熱湯で大根をゆで、続いてにんじんを加え、柔らかくなったら水けをきる。

3　しいたけは軸を取り、熱湯で3分ゆでて、水けをきる。

4　里芋は1cm厚さの輪切りにし、水から柔らかくなるまでゆでる。

5　三つ葉はさっと塩ゆでにし、水でさまし、水けを絞り、4cm長さに切る。

6　もちはあまり焦がさないように柔らかく焼く。→❶

7　だしを火にかけ、煮立ったら、みそを溶き入れ、鶏肉、野菜を加える。

8　器に鶏肉、野菜、三つ葉、もちを盛り、熱い汁をはり、ゆずをのせる。

❶

Soup with Rice Cakes
Ozōni

260 kcal per serving

◆ DIRECTIONS

1 Slice chicken into ⅛-inch thick strips, and parboil.

2 Cut *daikon* into quarter-rounds ⅛-inch thick, and carrot into quarter-rounds ¹/₁₆-inch thick. Cook *daikon* in boiling water, add carrot, boil until tender. Drain.

3 Cut off mushroom stems, cook the caps in boiling water 3 minutes. Drain.

4 Slice taro ⅜-inch thick, and place in a pot with cold water. Boil until tender.

5 Blanch *mitsuba* in salted boiling water. Rinse in cold water, squeeze out, and cut into 1½-inch lengths.

6 Broil rice cakes until tender. Do not brown.→❶

7 Bring *dashi* to a boil, add dissolved miso, chicken, and vegetables.

8 Place chicken, vegetables, *mitsuba*, and one rice cake in each bowl. Add hot broth, and top with *yuzu* citron rind.

◆ INGREDIENTS (4 servings)

4⅕ oz chicken breast
3½ oz *daikon* radish
1¾ oz carrot
4 fresh *shiitake* mushrooms
2 (3½ oz) taros (*satoimo*)
1 bunch (1¾ oz) *mitsuba* (trefoil)
4 *mochi* rice cakes
Soup
  2½ U.S. cups *dashi*
  4⅕ oz white miso
slivered *yuzu* citron rind

ご 飯

1人分　320 kcal

◆材　料 (4人分)

米　2カップ (360 g)
水　3カップ (600 cc)

◆米のとぎ方

1　米にたっぷりの水を入れて手早く混ぜ、濁り水はすぐに捨てる(さっと洗うのは、米が最初に出会った水分をすぐに吸収するので、1回目のぬか臭い水を吸わせないため)。

2　手のひらで押しつけるようにといで、水を加えてすすぐ。→❶

3　水を取り替えながら、水が澄むまで、くり返しよく洗う。

4　ざるに上げて水けをきり、30分おく(米に水分を充分に吸わせる)。→❷

◆釜や鍋での炊き方

1　ふたつきの厚手の鍋に洗い米と分量の水を入れ、中火にかける(約10分)。

2　沸騰してきたら1～2分強火にし、あと弱火で約15分炊く。

3　最後に30秒強火にし、火をとめる。

4　約10分蒸らす。

5　さっくりとほぐす。

◆炊飯器で炊く場合

1　ざるに上げておいた洗い米を入れ、定量の水を加えて炊く。

2　約10分蒸らす。

3　さっくりとほぐす。

❶

❷

Boiled Rice

Gohan

320 kcal per serving

◆ TO WASH RICE

1 Place rice in a bowl, add ample water, stir quickly, and discard the cloudy water immediately.
(Be sure to discard this first rinsing water, which smells of bran, as soon as possible, because rice will absorb the moisture quickly.)

2 Mix rice well so that the grains rub against each other, add water, and drain. →❶

3 Repeat until water is almost clear.

4 Drain in a sieve, and let stand for 30 minutes so rice absorbs moisture. →❷

◆ INGREDIENTS (4 servings)

12²/₃ oz medium grain rice
2¹/₂ U.S. cups water

◆ TO COOK RICE IN POTS OR PANS

1 Place rinsed rice and water in a heavy pot, cover, and heat on medium for 10 minutes.

2 When water boils, turn the heat high for 1 – 2 minutes, then turn down to low, and cook for 15 minutes.

3 Turn heat up high for 30 seconds, and remove from heat.

4 Let stand for 10 minutes.

5 Stir lightly.

◆ TO COOK RICE USING AN AUTOMATIC RICE COOKER

1 Transfer rinsed rice from sieve to rice cooker, add water, following machine's measure, and start cooking.

2 Let stand for 10 minutes.

3 Stir lightly.

かやくご飯

| 1人分　400 kcal |

◆材　料(4人分)

米　2カップ (360 g)
　だし　3カップ (600 cc)
　塩　小さじ½
　みりん　大さじ1
　薄口しょうゆ　大さじ3
鶏もも肉 (皮なし)　200 g
こんにゃく　50 g
生しいたけ　4枚
にんじん　50 g
三つ葉　½束 (25 g)
塩　少々

◆作り方

1　米はよく洗い、ざるに上げて30分おく。

2　鶏肉は1cm角に切り、さっと湯通しする。

3　こんにゃくは3cm長さの細切りにして、
さっとゆでる。

4　しいたけは軸を切って薄切りに、
にんじんは3cm長さの細切りにする。

5　三つ葉はさっと塩ゆでにし、水で
さまして水けをきり、3cm長さに切る。

6　鍋に米、調味しただし、三つ葉以外の
具を入れてさっと混ぜ、具を均等に散らし
て、炊く*。始めは中火にかける(約10分)。
沸騰してきたら1〜2分強火にし、中火の
弱で約15分炊く。最後に30秒強火にし、
火をとめる。

7　10分ほど蒸らし、三つ葉を加えて、
具が均一になるように混ぜる。

*[炊飯器]で炊く場合は、
定量の水を加えて炊く。

Rice with Chicken and Vegetables
Kayaku Gohan

400 kcal per serving

◆ DIRECTIONS

1 Wash rice carefully, drain in a sieve, and let stand for 30 minutes.

2 Cut chicken into ⅜-inch cubes, and briefly parboil.

3 Cut *konnyaku* into 1-inch thin strips, and briefly parboil.

4 Remove stems from *shiitake* mushrooms, and slice thinly.
Cut carrot into thin 1-inch strips.

5 Parboil *mitsuba* briefly in salted water, cool in cold water, and drain.
Cut into 1-inch lengths.

6 Place rice, *dashi* with seasonings, and all ingredients except *mitsuba* in a pot, mix lightly to spread chicken and vegetables, and cook.* Begin over medium heat for about 10 minutes. When boiling, raise heat to high for 1–2 minutes, then turn down to medium low, and cook for 15 minutes. Turn up heat to high again at the finish for 30 seconds, and remove from heat.

7 Let stand for about 10 minutes, add *mitsuba*, and mix so that rice, chicken, and vegetables are combined well.

* If using an automatic rice cooker, follow the machine's water measure.

◆ INGREDIENTS (4 servings)

12⅔ oz rice

- 2½ U.S. cups *dashi*
- ½ tsp salt
- 1 Tbsp *mirin*
- 3 Tbsp light soy sauce

7 oz chicken thighs, skinned

1¾ oz *konnyaku* (devil's tongue jelly)

4 fresh *shiitake* mushrooms

1¾ oz carrot

½ bunch (⅞ oz) *mitsuba* (trefoil)

pinch salt

栗ご飯

1人分　430 kcal

◆材　料 (4人分)

米　2カップ (360 g)
水　3カップ (600 cc)
塩　小さじ1
栗　15個 (400 g)

◆作り方

1　米はよく洗い、ざるに上げて
30分おく。

2　栗は水に30分～1時間ほどつける。

3　栗の底を切り落として、鬼皮をはぎとる
ようにむき、次にとがったほうに向けて、
渋皮をむく。6～8等分に切り、水に30分
さらす。→❶❷

4　分量の水に塩を溶かす。

5　鍋に米、栗、塩水を入れて炊く*。
始めは中火にかける（約10分）。沸騰して
きたら1～2分強火にし、あと弱火で
15～20分炊き、最後に30秒強火にして
火をとめる。

6　10分ほど蒸らし、さっくりと混ぜる。

＊[炊飯器]で炊く場合は、定量の水を加えて
炊く。

❶　　　　❷

Chestnut Rice
Kuri Gohan

430 kcal per serving

◆ DIRECTIONS

1 Wash rice well and drain in a sieve, let stand for 30 minutes.

2 Soak chestnuts in water for 30–60 minutes.

3 Cut off bottom portion of chestnut skin, tear off outer skin, and working from bottom to top, peel off inner skin. Cut chestnuts into 6–8 pieces, and soak again for 30 minutes.→❶❷

4 Dissolve salt in the water.

5 Place rice, chestnuts, and salted water in a pot and cook* over medium heat about 10 minutes. When boiling, turn heat up to high for 1–2 minutes, then turn down to low and cook for 15–20 minutes. Turn up heat to high again at the finish for 30 seconds, and remove from heat.

6 Let stand for about 10 minutes, and stir lightly.

* If using an automatic rice cooker, follow the machine's water measure.

◆ INGREDIENTS (4 servings)

12²/₃ oz rice
2¹/₂ U.S. cups water
1 tsp salt
15 (14 oz) chestnuts

豆ご飯

1人分　330 kcal

◆材　料 (4人分)

米　2カップ (360 g)
水　3カップ (600 cc)
塩　小さじ1
えんどう豆 (さやつき)
　　300 g (正味100 g)
塩　小さじ1

◆作り方

1　米はよく洗い、ざるに上げて
30分おく。

2　えんどう豆はさやから出し、塩で
もみ洗いし、水洗いして、水けをきる。→❶

3　分量の水に塩を溶かす。

4　鍋に米、えんどう豆、塩水を入れて
炊く*。中火にかける (約10分)。沸騰して
きたら1〜2分強火にし、弱火で15〜20分
炊く。最後に30秒強火にし、火をとめる。

5　10分ほど蒸らし、さっくりと混ぜる。

＊[炊飯器]で炊く場合は、定量の水を加えて
炊く。

❶

Green Pea Rice

Mame Gohan

330 kcal per serving

◆ DIRECTIONS

1 Wash rice well and drain in a sieve. Let stand for 30 minutes.

2 Shell peas, rub well with salt, rinse, and drain.→❶

3 Dissolve salt in the water.

4 Place rice, peas, and salted water in a pot and cook* over medium heat about 10 minutes. When boiling, turn heat up to high for 1–2 minutes, then turn down to low and cook for 15–20 minutes. Turn heat up again to high at the finish for 30 seconds, and remove from heat.

5 Let stand for about 10 minutes, and stir lightly.

*If using an automatic rice cooker, follow the machine's water measure.

◆ INGREDIENTS (4 servings)

12²/₃ oz rice

2¹/₂ U.S. cups water

l tsp salt

10¹/₂ oz green peas in pods
    (3¹/₂ oz peas)

l tsp salt

赤飯

1人分 520 kcal

◆材　料(4人分)

もち米　2カップ (400 g)
あずき　1カップ (150 g)
酒塩
　酒　100 cc
　塩　小さじ½
ごま塩
　黒ごま　小さじ1
　塩　小さじ1

◆作り方

1　もち米は洗って、12時間水につける。

2　あずきは洗って、水を入れて、強火で5分煮て、ゆで汁を捨てる。

3　新しい水5カップを入れ、再び火にかけ、沸騰したら弱火にして柔らかくなるまでゆでる。ざるに上げ、ゆで汁は別にさます。→❶

4　さめたゆで汁にもち米を1時間つけ、布巾を敷いたざるに上げて水けをきる。

5　蒸気の上がった蒸し器に布巾ごともち米を移して、強火で約30分蒸す。途中、酒塩を2〜3度ふりかける。→❷❸

6　あずきを上にのせて、温まる程度に蒸す。

7　小鍋で黒ごまをいり、塩を加えてさらにいってごま塩を作る。

8　器に赤飯を盛り、ごま塩をふる。

メモ
• 祝い事のときに食べるご飯。

❶

❷

❸

Red Rice
with *Azuki* Beans

Seki-han

520 kcal per serving

◆ DIRECTIONS

1 Wash glutinous rice and soak in water for 12 hours.

2 Wash *azuki* beans, boil over high heat for 5 minutes, and discard water.

3 Add 5 cups of fresh water to the pot of beans over heat. When it boils, turn down the heat to low, and cook beans until tender. Drain in a sieve, reserving hot water in a bowl. Allow water to cool. →❶

4 Soak rice in the cool bean water for 1 hour, and drain in a sieve lined with cheesecloth.

5 Transfer the rice with the cheesecloth to a steamer, and cook over high heat for 30 minutes. Sprinkle with salted *saké* a couple of times during cooking. →❷❸

6 Place *azuki* beans on top of rice, and steam to heat beans.

7 Toast black sesame seeds in a small pan, add salt, and continue toasting to make sesame salt.

8 Serve red rice sprinkled with sesame salt.

NOTE
• Red rice is eaten for celebration.

◆ INGREDIENTS (4 servings)

14 oz glutinous rice
5 1/4 oz *azuki* beans
Salted *Saké*
  { 3 1/3 oz *saké*
  { 1/2 tsp salt
Sesame Salt
  { 1 tsp black sesame seeds
  { 1 tsp salt

親子丼

1人分　690 kcal

◆材　料(4人分)

米　2カップ (360 g)

鶏もも肉 (皮なし)

　　1枚 (400 g)

玉ねぎ　½個 (70 g)

青ねぎ　2本

煮汁

　だし　500 cc

　砂糖　大さじ3

　みりん　大さじ3

　しょうゆ　大さじ4

　薄口しょうゆ　大さじ4

卵　8個

◆作り方

1　ご飯を炊く(48頁参照)。

2　鶏肉は2cm角に切り、玉ねぎは薄切り、青ねぎは斜め切りにする。

3　鍋に煮汁の材料を入れて煮立て、鶏肉をさっと煮る。

4　1人分ずつ作る。小さな鍋に煮汁と具を¼量ずつ入れて煮立て、卵2個を溶いて回し入れ、鍋を動かしながら、さっと混ぜて半熟程度まで煮る。→❶

5　器に温かいご飯を盛り、形をくずさないように上にのせる。

❶

Chicken-'n'-Egg on Rice

Oyako-don

690 kcal per serving

◆ DIRECTIONS

1 Cook rice according to page 49.

2 Cut chicken into ³⁄₄-inch cubes. Cut onions into thin slices, and chop scallions diagonally.

3 Place all sauce ingredients in a pan, bring to a boil, add chicken, and boil briefly.

4 Prepare toppings individually. Place ¹⁄₄ of the sauce, chicken, and vegetables in a small pot, and bring to a boil. Beat 2 eggs, pour over in circular motion, and cook until egg is half done, stirring and moving the pot. →❶

5 Place a portion of hot rice in a bowl, and slide chicken and egg topping carefully over rice.

◆ INGREDIENTS (4 servings)

12²⁄₃ oz rice
14 oz chicken thigh, boned and skinned
¹⁄₂ (2¹⁄₂ oz) onion
2 scallions
Sauce
  2¹⁄₈ U.S. cups *dashi*
  3 Tbsp sugar
  3 Tbsp *mirin*
  4 Tbsp soy sauce
  4 Tbsp light soy sauce
8 eggs

牛丼

1人分 700 kcal

◆材　料 (4人分)

米　2カップ (360 g)
牛ロース肉 (薄切り)　400 g
玉ねぎ　1個 (150 g)
三つ葉　1束 (50 g)
煮汁
　┌ だし　300 cc
　│ 酒　100 cc
　┤ 砂糖　大さじ3
　│ みりん　大さじ2
　└ しょうゆ　大さじ5

◆作り方

1　ご飯を炊く(48頁参照)。

2　牛肉は5cm長さに切る。
玉ねぎは縦半分に切って薄切りし、
三つ葉は2cm長さに切る。

3　鍋に煮汁の材料を合わせて煮立て、
牛肉と玉ねぎを入れて3分ほど煮る。

4　火をとめる直前に三つ葉を加える。

5　器に温かいご飯を盛り、上にのせる。

Beef Bowl

Gyū-don

700 kcal per serving

◆ DIRECTIONS

1 Cook rice according to page 49.

2 Cut beef into 2-inch pieces.
Cut onion in half lengthwise and
slice thinly. Cut *mitsuba* into ¾-inch
lengths.

3 Place all sauce ingredients in a skillet,
bring to a boil, add beef and onion, and
cook for about 3 minutes.

4 Add *mitsuba* just before removing
from heat.

5 Place hot rice in bowls, and transfer
beef topping onto rice.

◆ INGREDIENTS (4 servings)

12⅔ oz rice
14 oz beef loin, thinly sliced
1 (5¼ oz) onion
1 bunch (1¾ oz) *mitsuba*
  (trefoil)
Sauce
  ⌈ 10 oz *dashi*
  │ 3⅓ oz *saké*
  ⦃ 3 Tbsp sugar
  │ 2 Tbsp *mirin*
  ⌊ 5 Tbsp soy sauce

天丼

1人分　550 kcal

◆材　料 (4人分)

米　2カップ (360 g)
えび (30 gの無頭)　8尾
生しいたけ　4枚
青じそ　4枚
てんだし
　┌ だし　120 cc
　│ みりん　大さじ3
　└ しょうゆ　大さじ3
衣
　┌ 卵　1個
　│ 冷水　120 cc
　│ 小麦粉　50 g
　└ コーンスターチ　30 g
小麦粉　適量
揚げ油　適量

◆作り方

1　ご飯を炊く (48頁参照)。

2　えびは背わたを取り、尾を残し殻を
むく。尾先を切り、包丁の先でしごいて
水を出す。腹に切り目を数ヵ所入れ、
押さえるようにして筋をのばす。→❶

3　しいたけ、青じそは軸を切る。

4　鍋にてんだしの材料を合わせ、
一煮立ちさせる。

5　衣を作る。卵と冷水を混ぜ、小麦粉と
コーンスターチを合わせたものを入れて、
さっくり混ぜる。

6　揚げ油を175℃に熱し、えび、しいたけ、
青じそに小麦粉を薄くまぶして、衣を
つけて揚げる。

7　ご飯を盛り、揚げたての天ぷらをのせ、
てんだしをかける。

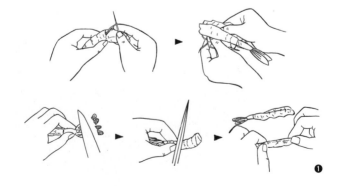

❶

Tempura Bowl

Ten-don

550 kcal per serving

◆ DIRECTIONS

1 Cook rice according to page 49.

2 Devein shrimp, and shell, leaving tails. Cut off the tip of tails, and force out any moisture with the back of a knife. Score underside of shrimp at several places to flatten. →❶

3 Trim stems from *shiitake* mushrooms and *shiso* leaves.

4 Place tempura sauce ingredients in a pan and bring to a boil.

5 To make batter, combine eggs and ice water in a bowl, add flour combined with cornstarch, and mix lightly.

6 Preheat oil to 350°F. Dust shrimp, *shiitake*, and *shiso* leaves lightly with flour, coat with batter, and deep-fry.

7 Transfer tempura onto hot rice in bowls, and pour sauce over.

◆ INGREDIENTS (4 servings)

12²/₃ oz rice
8 shrimp in shells without heads, 1 oz each
4 fresh *shiitake* mushrooms
4 green *shiso* leaves
Tempura Sauce
 ⎡ ¹/₂ U.S. cup *dashi*
 ⎨ 3 Tbsp *mirin*
 ⎣ 3 Tbsp soy sauce
Batter
 ⎡ 1 egg
 ⎨ ¹/₂ U.S. cup ice water
 ⎪ 1³/₄ oz flour
 ⎣ 1 oz cornstarch
flour
oil for deep-frying

カツ丼

1人分　960 kcal

◆材　料 (4人分)

米　2カップ (360 g)
とんカツ (→192頁)　4枚
玉ねぎ　½個 (70 g)
三つ葉　1束 (50 g)
卵　4個
煮汁
  だし　400 cc
  みりん　100 cc
  砂糖　大さじ1
  しょうゆ　大さじ4

◆作り方

1　ご飯を炊く(48頁参照)。

2　とんカツは2cm幅に切る。

3　玉ねぎは薄切り、三つ葉は2cm長さに切る。

4　鍋にみりんを入れて一煮立ちさせ、だし、砂糖、しょうゆを加えて再び煮立てる。

5　1人分ずつ作る。材料を4等分し、小さい鍋に玉ねぎと煮汁を入れて3分煮、三つ葉、とんカツを加え、さっと煮て、卵1個を溶き、回し入れてとじる。

6　器にご飯を盛り、上にのせる。

Pork Cutlet Bowl

Katsu-don

960 kcal per serving

◆ DIRECTIONS

1 Cook rice according to page 49.

2 Cut pork cutlets into ¾-inch wide strips.

3 Cut onion into thin slices, *mitsuba* into ¾-inch lenghs.

4 Place *mirin* in a saucepan, bring to a boil, add *dashi*, sugar, and soy sauce, and bring back to boil.

5 Make 1 serving at a time.
Divide ingredients into 4 portions.
Place onion and sauce in a small skillet and cook for 3 minutes, add *mitsuba* and pork cutlet, cook quickly.
Add beaten egg in a circular motion, and cook until the egg is half done.

6 Slide the cutlet topping onto hot rice in a bowl.

◆ INGREDIENTS (4 servings)

12⅔ oz rice
4 pork cutlets (→p. 193)
½ (2½ oz) onion
1 bunch (1¾ oz) *mitsuba* (trefoil)
4 eggs
Sauce
  ⎡ 1⅔ U.S. cups *dashi*
  ⎢ 1⅔ oz *mirin*
  ⎢ 1 Tbsp sugar
  ⎣ 4 Tbsp soy sauce

そぼろ丼

◆材　料(4人分)

米　2カップ (360 g)

鶏そぼろ
> 鶏ひき肉 (脂身の少ない
> もの)　300 g
> 酒　大さじ5
> 砂糖　大さじ2
> みりん　大さじ3
> しょうゆ　大さじ5
> しょうがの絞り汁　小さじ1

卵そぼろ
> 卵　4個
> みりん　大さじ3
> 砂糖　大さじ1
> 塩　小さじ½

グリーンピース (水煮)
　大さじ2

◆作り方

1　ご飯を炊く(48頁参照)。

2　鍋にひき肉、調味料、しょうがの絞り汁を入れてよく混ぜ合わせ、いりつけるように火を通す。

3　卵は溶きほぐし、調味料を混ぜ合わせて火にかけ、数本の箸でかき混ぜながら、水分が少し残る状態になるまでいる。→❶

4　グリーンピースは熱湯でさっとゆでる。

5　ご飯の上に各そぼろを半々盛り、グリーンピースを散らす。

❶

Minced Chicken and Egg Bowl

Soboro-don

690 kcal per serving

◆ DIRECTIONS

1 Cook rice according to page 49.

2 Place ground chicken, seasonings and ginger juice in a skillet, mix well, and brown, stirring.

3 Beat eggs, mix with seasonings, and cook in a skillet, stirring with chopsticks. Cook until moisture is almost gone. → ❶

4 Parboil green peas briefly.

5 Arrange chicken and egg toppings side by side on hot rice in bowls, making 2 "patches," and sprinkle with green peas.

◆ INGREDIENTS (4 servings)

12²/₃ oz rice

Minced Chicken Topping
- 10½ oz lean ground chicken
- 5 Tbsp *saké*
- 2 Tbsp sugar
- 3 Tbsp *mirin*
- 5 Tbsp soy sauce
- 1 tsp fresh ginger juice

Egg Topping
- 4 eggs
- 3 Tbsp *mirin*
- 1 Tbsp sugar
- ½ tsp salt

2 Tbsp boiled green peas

さけの混ぜご飯

1人分　410 kcal

◆**材　料**(4人分)

米　2カップ (360 g)
塩ざけ (100 gのもの)
　2切れ
青じそ　8枚
焼きのり　1枚
しば漬け* (みじん切り)
　大さじ2
白いりごま　大さじ2

*なす、しょうが、みょうがを
赤じその葉とともに刻んで
塩漬けにした京都特産の
漬け物。

◆**作り方**

1　ご飯を炊く(48頁参照)。

2　塩ざけは両面をこんがりと焼き、
熱いうちに細かくほぐす。骨と皮は除く。

3　青じそはせん切りにして、水にさらし、
水けをきる。→❶

4　焼きのりは細かくちぎる。

5　ご飯に塩ざけ、しば漬け、ごまを
混ぜ合わせる。

6　器に盛り、のり、青じそを散らす。

❶

Salmon and Pickle Rice

Sake no Maze-gohan

410 kcal per serving

◆ DIRECTIONS

1 Cook rice according to page 49.

2 Broil both sides of the salted salmon, and flake into small pieces. Discard bones and skin.

3 Cut *shiso* leaves into fine strips, soak in cold water, and drain. →❶

4 Tear *nori* seaweed into small pieces.

5 Combine hot rice, salted salmon, *shibazuke* pickles, and sesame seeds, and mix well.

6 Serve in bowls with *nori* and *shiso* leaves sprinkled on top.

◆ INGREDIENTS (4 servings)

12²/₃ oz rice

2 slices salted salmon, 3¹/₂ oz each

8 green *shiso* leaves

1 sheet *nori* seaweed, toasted

2 Tbsp minced *shibazuke* pickles*

2 Tbsp white sesame seeds, toasted

Shibazuke is a type of pickle from the Kyoto region, consisting of chopped eggplant, ginger, *myoga*, and red *shiso* leaves.

かに雑炊

1人分 290 kcal

◆材　料 (4人分)

ご飯 (炊きたて)*
　茶わん4杯分 (400 g)
かに (缶詰)　200 g
なめこ　1袋 (50 g)
卵　4個
三つ葉　½束 (25 g)
雑炊のだし
　だし　1000 cc
　みりん　大さじ2
　塩　小さじ2
　薄口しょうゆ　大さじ3
しょうがの絞り汁　大さじ1

*冷やご飯を使うとき:
ざるに入れて水で洗い、
粘りをとる。

◆作り方

1　かには軟骨を取り除いてほぐす。

2　なめこは熱湯でさっとゆでる。

3　卵は溶きほぐし、三つ葉は3cm長さに切る。

4　鍋にだしと調味料を入れ、一煮立ちしたらご飯、かに、なめこを加える。
再び煮立ったら中火にして2〜3分煮る。

5　三つ葉、しょうがの絞り汁を加え、溶き卵を流し入れ、半熟になったらふたをして火をとめる。

Crab Risotto
Kani Zōsui

290 kcal per serving

◆ DIRECTIONS

1 Discard white tendons from crabmeat, and flake meat into pieces.

2 Parboil *nameko* mushrooms briefly.

3 Beat eggs. Cut *mitsuba* into 1-inch lengths.

4 Place *dashi* and seasonings in a pot, bring to a boil. Add rice, crabmeat, and *nameko* mushrooms. When it boils for the second time, turn heat down to medium, and cook for 2–3 minutes.

5 Add *mitsuba* and ginger juice, and pour in beaten eggs in a circular motion. When egg is half done, cover and remove from heat.

◆ INGREDIENTS (4 servings)

4 rice bowls (14 oz) hot cooked rice*

7 oz canned crabmeat

1 pack (1¾ oz) *nameko* mushrooms

4 eggs

½ bunch (⅞ oz) *mitsuba* (trefoil)

Risotto *Dashi*

- 4 U.S. cups *dashi*
- 2 Tbsp *mirin*
- 2 tsp salt
- 3 Tbsp light soy sauce

1 Tbsp fresh ginger juice

∗When using cold cooked rice, rinse the rice with water in a sieve to get rid of the stickiness.

たい茶漬け

1人分　310 kcal

◆材　料(4人分)

ご飯 (炊きたて)
　茶わん4杯分 (400 g)
たい (上身、皮なし)　300 g
漬け地
　┌ 白いりごま　大さじ4
　│ 酒 (煮きり)＊　大さじ1
　│ みりん (煮きり)＊　大さじ1
　└ しょうゆ　大さじ3
焼きのり　1枚
わさび　適量
せん茶　適量

＊煮切り：酒やみりんを煮立て、アルコール分を燃やして、抜いたもの。

◆作り方

1　白いりごまはすり鉢で半ずりにし、調味料を加え、混ぜ合わせる。→❶

2　たいは薄いそぎ切りにして、合わせた漬け地に15分漬ける。→❷❸

3　焼きのりは細かくちぎる。

4　わさびは小さじ2ほどおろす(116頁参照)。(市販品の粉わさび、冷凍おろしわさびでも可)。

5　ご飯を盛り、たいを並べて、のりをのせ、わさびを中央におく。

6　熱いせん茶を注ぎ、ふたをして1〜2分蒸らす。

❶

❷

❸

Tea and Rice with Sea Bream

Tai Cha-zuke

310 kcal per serving

◆ DIRECTIONS

1 Grind toasted white sesame seeds roughly in a mortar, add seasonings, and mix well. →❶

2 Cut sea bream fillet into thin strips, and marinate for 15 minutes. →❷❸

3 Tear *nori* seaweed into small pieces.

4 Grate *wasabi* about 2 tsp. See page 117. (Powdered, tubed, or frozen *wasabi* is also available.)

5 Serve hot rice in bowls, arrange sea bream on rice, scatter *nori* seaweed over top, and place a small mound of grated *wasabi* in the center.

6 Fill with hot green tea, cover, and let stand for 1–2 minutes.

◆ INGREDIENTS (4 servings)

4 rice bowls (14 oz) hot cooked rice
10½ oz sea bream fillet, skinned
Marinade
  ⎰ 4 Tbsp white sesame seeds, toasted
  ⎱ 1 Tbsp boiled *saké* *
    1 Tbsp boiled *mirin* *
    3 Tbsp soy sauce
1 sheet *nori* seaweed, toasted
wasabi horseradish
green tea

*boiled *saké* or *mirin*: boiling burns off the alcohol

すし飯

1人分 350 kcal

◆材　料(4人分)

米　2カップ (360 g)

水　560 cc

昆布　5 cm

すし酢

　酢　大さじ4

　砂糖　大さじ3

　塩　小さじ1½

◆作り方

1 米はよく洗い、ざるに上げ、30分おく。

2 鍋に洗い米、分量の水（普通の
ご飯より水はひかえめ）、昆布を入れて
炊く(48頁参照)。

3 すし酢の材料をよく混ぜ合わせる。

4 炊き上がったご飯を飯台（すしおけ）へ
山盛りにあけ、すし酢を回しかけ、
ご飯を切るように手早く混ぜ、うちわなど
であおいでさます。

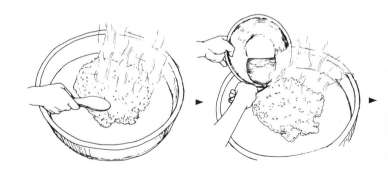

Sushi Rice
Sushi-meshi

350 kcal per serving

◆ DIRECTIONS

1 Wash rice carefully, drain in a sieve, and let stand for 30 minutes.

2 Place rinsed rice, water*, and *konbu* in a pot, and cook rice according to page 49.

3 Stir together all sushi vinegar ingredients.

4 Transfer hot rice to a large wooden sushi bowl, making a mound. Pour sushi vinegar over, and mix rice by cutting across it in a fast slashing motion, then cool it by fanning.

∗ The amount of water for cooking sushi rice is a little less than that used in cooking regular rice.

◆ INGREDIENTS (4 servings)

12²/₃ oz rice
19 oz water
2-inch square *konbu* kelp
Sushi Vinegar
  ⎰ 4 Tbsp rice vinegar
  ⎱ 3 Tbsp sugar
    1¹/₂ tsp salt

にぎりずし

1人分 690 kcal

◆材料(4人分)

すし飯 (→74頁)　800 g
えび (30 gの無頭)　8尾
まぐろ (上身)　200 g
たい (上身、皮なし)　200 g
いか (上身)　150 g
うに　40かけ
卵焼き (→86頁)　8切れ
手酢
　水　200 cc
　酢　大さじ1
焼きのり　1枚
おろしわさび (→116頁)　適量
しょうゆ　適量
しょうがの甘酢漬け
　(→114頁)　適量

❷

❶

◆作り方

1　すし飯を用意する。

2　えびは背わたを抜き、串を刺し、熱湯で塩ゆでし、水にとり、串を抜く。尾を残して殻をむき、腹開きにする。→❶❷

3　まぐろは2.5cm×6cm角、5mm厚さに切る。たい、いか、卵焼きも同じ大きさに切る。

4　手に手酢をつける。左手にねたを持ち、右手にすし飯を約20gとってまとめる。すし飯を持ったまま、人差し指でおろしわさびをとり、ねたの裏側につけて、すし飯をのせる。ねたごとすし飯を四方から押さえて形を整える。返してねたを上にして持ち、もう一度押さえて形を整える。まぐろ、たい、いか、えび、卵焼きをにぎる。卵焼きのにぎりは細く切ったのりで中心を巻く。にぎり方は78頁参照。

5　うにはにぎったすし飯の回りに3cm×12cmに切ったのりを巻きつけ、おろしわさびをのせ、うにをのせる。

6　器に盛りつけ、しょうゆ、しょうがの甘酢漬けを添える。

Nigiri Sushi

Nigiri-zushi

690 kcal per serving

◆ DIRECTIONS

1 Prepare sushi rice.

2 Devein and skewer shrimp, parboil in salted water, transfer to cold water, and remove the skewers. Shell, leaving tails, and slit open the underside of the shrimp.→❶❷

3 Cut tuna fillet, sea bream, squid, and rolled omelette into 1 × 2½ × ⅛-inch pieces.

4 Moisten your hands with hand vinegar. Holding a topping in the left hand, take a small amount of rice (⅔ oz) in your right hand, and shape rice into small rectangular block. Holding rice in your right hand, scoop up a small amount of grated *wasabi* using your right index finger, spread it on the back of the topping, and place rice rectangle on the topping. Shape by pressing sides. Then turn and press top to finish shaping. Repeat this with tuna, sea bream, squid, shrimp, and rolled omelette toppings. Secure rolled omelette sushi with a thin band of *nori* seaweed. See page 78.

5 To make sea urchin sushi, shape rice, and ring lengthwise with a 1 × 4½-inch strip of *nori* seaweed. Season the top of the rice with *wasabi*, and top with sea urchin.

6 Arrange on plates, and serve with soy sauce and sweet-vinegared ginger.

◆ INGREDIENTS (4 servings)

28 oz sushi rice (→p. 75)
8 shrimp in shells without heads, 1 oz each
7 oz tuna fillet
7 oz sea bream fillet, skinned
5¼ oz squid (body only)
40 sea urchin segments
8 slices rolled omelette (→p. 87)
Hand Vinegar
  ⎰ 6⅔ oz water
  ⎱ 1 Tbsp vinegar
1 sheet *nori* seaweed, toasted (→p. 117)
grated *wasabi* horseradish
soy sauce
sweet-vinegared ginger (→p. 115)

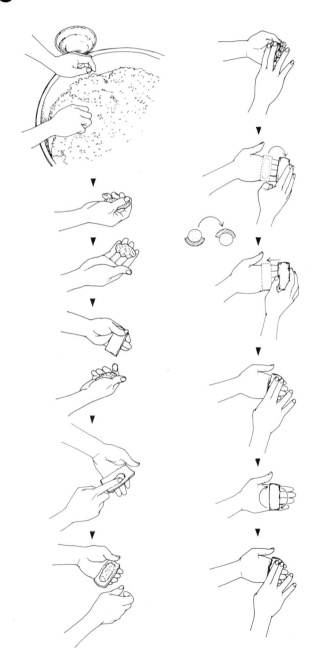

手巻きずし

1人分 610 kcal

◆材　料(4人分)

すし飯(→74頁)　800 g

まぐろ(上身)　120 g

いか納豆
- いか(細切り)　100 g
- 納豆　大さじ4
- さらしねぎ　小さじ2
- しょうゆ　小さじ1
- 練りがらし　小さじ¼

かにマヨネーズ
- かにの身(缶詰)　150 g
- マヨネーズ　大さじ2

きゅうり　½本

アボカド　½個

たくあん　50 g

青じそ　8枚

焼きのり　20枚

しょうゆ　適量

おろしわさび(→116頁)　適量

しょうがの甘酢漬け
　(→114頁)　適量

◆作り方

1　すし飯を用意する。

2　まぐろは細い棒状に切る。

3　納豆は粗く刻み、しょうゆ、からしで
調味し、いか、さらしねぎを加えて混ぜる。

4　かにはマヨネーズであえる。

5　きゅうり、アボカドは細い棒状に切る。
たくあんは5cm長さのせん切りにする。
青じそは軸を切る。

6　焼きのりは½枚の長方形に切る。

7　器にすし飯、ねた*、薬味、のりを
盛りつける。

8　のりにすし飯を適量広げ、好みの具を
巻きながら食べる。しょうゆ、おろしわさび、
しょうがの甘酢漬けを添える。

*ねたはたい、いか、たこ、えび、うに、イクラ、
卵焼きなども。

Do-It-Yourself Sushi Rolls

Temaki-zushi

610 kcal per serving

◆ DIRECTIONS

1 Prepare sushi rice.

2 Cut tuna into thin strips.

3 Mince *natto* coarsely, season with soy sauce and mustard, add squid and rinsed scallions, and mix.

4 Mix crabmeat and mayonnaise.

5 Cut cucumber and avocado into thin sticks. Cut *takuan* pickle finely into 2-inch lengths. Trim stems off *shiso* leaves.

6 Cut *nori* sheets in half to make rectangles.

7 Arrange rice, ingredients*, condiments, and *nori* sheets on serving plates.

8 Help yourself to rice and ingredients. Spread rice on a *nori* sheet, take any ingredients and make a sushi roll to eat. Serve with soy sauce, grated *wasabi* horseradish, and sweet-vinegared ginger.

 *Sea bream, squid, octopus, shrimp, sea urchin, salmon roe, and rolled omelette are also recommended.

◆ INGREDIENTS (4 servings)

28 oz sushi rice (→p. 75)
4 1/5 oz tuna fillet
squid and *natto* beans
  ⎰ **3 1/2 oz squid,**
     thinly sliced
    4 Tbsp *natto* beans
    2 tsp rinsed scallions
    I tsp soy sauce
  ⎱ **1/4 tsp mustard**
crabmeat and mayonnaise
  ⎰ **5 1/4 oz canned crabmeat**
  ⎱ **2 Tbsp mayonnaise**
1/2 cucumber
1/2 avocado
1 3/4 oz *takuan* pickle
8 green *shiso* leaves
20 sheets *nori* seaweed,
  toasted
soy sauce
grated *wasabi* horseradish
  (→p. 117)
sweet-vinegared ginger
  (→p. 115)

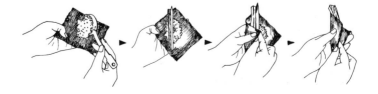

ばらずし

1人分 580 kcal

◆材 料(4人分)

すし飯(→74頁) 800 g

しいたけの甘煮

　干ししいたけ 4枚
　だし 150 cc
　砂糖、みりん 各大さじ1
　しょうゆ 大さじ2

薄焼き卵(＝錦糸卵)

　卵 2個
　塩 少々
　サラダ油 適量

えび(30 gの塩ゆで) 4尾
絹さや(塩ゆで) 8枚
焼きあなご 2本(180 g)
ちくわ 2本(120 g)

◆作り方

1 すし飯を用意する。

2 干ししいたけは水(またはぬるま湯)に
つけてもどし、軸を切り、水けを絞る。
鍋にだしと調味料を合わせ、しいたけを
加えて煮汁がほぼなくなるまで煮込み、
細切りにする。

3 卵は溶きほぐし、塩を混ぜて、こす。
温めた卵焼き鍋に卵液を少量流し、
全体に広げ、表面が乾いたら、裏返して
裏面もさっと焼く。3〜4枚焼き、さます。
2〜3等分に切って、せん切りにする。→❶

4 えび、絹さや、あなごは1cm幅の
ざく切りにする。

5 ちくわは刻み、すし飯に混ぜ合わせ、
具を彩りよく散らす。

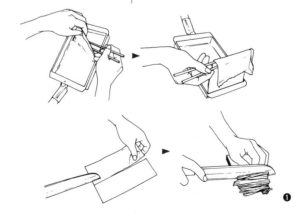

❶

Scattered Sushi
Bara-zushi

580 kcal per serving

◆ DIRECTIONS

1 Prepare sushi rice.

2 Soak dried *shiitake* mushrooms in cold or lukewarm water, remove stems, and squeeze out water. Combine *dashi* and seasonings in a pot, add s*hiitake*, and simmer until sauce is almost gone. Slice *shiitake* mushrooms thinly.

3 Beat eggs, add pinch salt, and strain. Heat a square omelette pan, pour in a small amount of egg and spread evenly. When surface is dry, turn over, and cook briefly. Make 3–4 sheets, and cool. Cut into 2–3 portions, and slice into fine strips.→❶

4 Cut shrimp, snow peas and grilled eels roughly into about ⅜-inch wide pieces.

5 Chop *chikuwa* into small pieces, combine with sushi rice, and mix. Scatter rest of ingredients to decorate colorfully.

◆ INGREDIENTS (4 servings)

28 oz sushi rice (→p. 75)

Simmered *Shiitake* Mushrooms

- 4 dried *shiitake* mushrooms
- 5 oz *dashi*
- 1 Tbsp sugar
- 1 Tbsp *mirin*
- 2 Tbsp soy sauce

Thin Omelette

- 2 eggs
- pinch salt
- dash vegetable oil

4 shrimp, boiled in salted water, 1 oz each

8 snow peas, boiled in salted water

2 (6¼ oz) grilled *anago* eel fillets

2 (4⅕ oz) *chikuwa* fishcake tubes

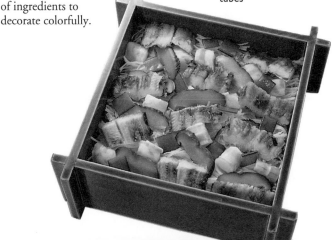

いなりずし

1人分 670 kcal

◆材　料 (4人分)

すし飯 (→74頁)　800 g
黒いりごま　大さじ2
油揚げ (正方形)　10枚
煮汁
[だし　400 cc
  砂糖　大さじ3
  みりん　大さじ1
  しょうゆ　大さじ3
しょうがの甘酢漬け
　(→114頁)　適量

◆作り方

1　油揚げは斜め半分の三角形に切り、熱湯でゆでて油抜きし、水けをふき取る。切り口を開いて袋状にする。→❶

2　鍋に煮汁の材料を入れ、一煮立ちさせる。

3　油揚げを加えて、落としぶたをして中火で煮汁が少量になるまで煮つめ、そのままさまして味を含ませる。

4　すし飯にいりごまを混ぜる。

5　油揚げを軽く絞り、すし飯を軽くにぎって詰める。両端を折り込み、側面を両側から指ではさむようにして三角形にする。→❷❸

6　器に盛りつけ、しょうがの甘酢漬けを添える。

メ　モ
・縦半分に切って四角形にしたり、裏返して使うと変化がつく。

❶

❷

Sushi Pockets

Inari-zushi

670 kcal per serving

◆ DIRECTIONS

1 Cut deep-fried tofu squares into triangles, parboil to remove excess oil, drain, and pat dry. Carefully open up tofu from cut side to make pouches. →❶

2 Combine sauce ingredients in a pot, bring to a boil.

3 Add deep-fried tofu, cover with a drop-lid, and simmer over medium heat until most of the sauce is gone.
Let stand to cool.

4 Combine sesame seeds with sushi rice and mix.

5 Squeeze out tofu pouches lightly, and stuff with sushi rice. Fold edges of pouch over rice, and press sides with fingers to make a triangular shape. →❷❸

6 Arrange on plates with sweet-vinegared ginger.

◆ INGREDIENTS (4 servings)

28 oz sushi rice (→p. 75)
2 Tbsp black sesame
  seeds, toasted
10 squares "thin"
  deep-fried tofu (*aburaage*)
Simmering Sauce
  ⎧ 1²/₃ U.S. cups *dashi*
  ⎪ 3 Tbsp sugar
  ⎨ 1 Tbsp *mirin*
  ⎩ 3 Tbsp soy sauce
sweet-vinegared ginger
  (→p. 115)

NOTE
• For variation, cut tofu squares in half to make rectangles, or turn pouches inside out.

❸

太巻きずし

1人分 720 kcal

◆材　料(4人分)

すし飯 (→74頁)　800 g

うなぎのかば焼き
　1本 (100 g)

しいたけの甘煮
　(→82頁) 8枚

高野豆腐の含め煮
　(→168頁) 2枚

かんぴょう旨煮
- かんぴょう　30 g
- だし　600 cc
- 砂糖　大さじ2
- みりん、しょうゆ
　　各大さじ3

卵焼き
- 卵　3個
- だし　大さじ2
- みりん　小さじ1
- しょうゆ　小さじ1
- 塩　小さじ1/4

サラダ油　適量

三つ葉　2束 (100 g)

塩　適量

焼きのり　4枚

◆作り方

1　うなぎは縦に四つ割りにする。
しいたけの甘煮は薄切りにする。
高野豆腐の含め煮は1枚を5等分に切り、
汁けを軽く絞る。

2　かんぴょうは塩でもみ洗いし、水に
1時間つけてもどし、たっぷりの熱湯で
15分ゆでる。鍋に煮汁の材料を合わせ、
かんぴょうを入れ、落としぶたをして、
弱火で30分煮る。

3　卵は溶きほぐし、だし、調味料を混ぜ
合わせて焼く(焼き方は140頁参照)。
あら熱をとり、1.5cm角の細長い棒状に
切る。

4　三つ葉は塩ゆでにし、冷水にさらし、
かたく絞る。

5　巻き簀の上に焼きのりを置き、
向こう側を3cm残してすし飯を広げる。
うなぎ、しいたけ、卵焼き、かんぴょう、
高野豆腐、三つ葉を1/4量ずつのせて、
手前から具を押さえながら一気に巻く。

6　1本を8つに切り分け、器に盛りつける。

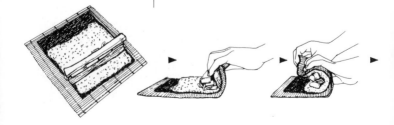

Thick-Rolled Sushi
Futo-maki-zushi

720 kcal per serving

◆ DIRECTIONS

1 Cut eel fillet into 4 strips lengthwise. Slice simmered *shiitake* thinly. Cut each *koya-dofu* cake into 5 portions, and lightly wring out excess moisture.

2 Rub gourd ribbons with salt to clean, soak in water for 1 hour, and boil in ample water for 15 minutes. Combine sauce ingredients, add gourd ribbons, cover with a drop-lid, and simmer over low heat for 30 minutes.

3 Beat eggs, add *dashi* and seasonings, and follow page 141 to make rolled omelette. When omelette cools down slightly, cut into long sticks about ¹/₂-inch wide.

4 Parboil *mitsuba* in lightly salted water, rinse in cold water, and wring out.

5 Place a sheet of *nori* seaweed on a bamboo rolling mat, spread with rice, leaving 1¹/₂-inch wide space empty on the side away from you. Lay out ¹/₄ of eel, *shiitake*, rolled omelette, *koya-dofu*, and *mitsuba*, and roll up all the way, holding ingredients in place.

6 Cut each roll into 8 portions, and arrange on serving plates.

◆ INGREDIENTS (4 servings)

28 oz sushi rice (→p. 75)
1 (3¹/₂ oz) grilled *unagi* eel
8 simmered s*hiitake* mushrooms (→p. 83)
2 cakes simmered *koya-dofu* (→p. 169)
Simmered Gourd Ribbons
- 1 oz *kanpyo* gourd ribbons
- 2 ¹/₂ U.S. cups *dashi*
- 2 Tbsp sugar
- 3 Tbsp *mirin*
- 3 Tbsp soy sauce

Rolled Omelette
- 3 eggs
- 2 Tbsp *dashi*
- 1 tsp *mirin*
- 1 tsp soy sauce
- ¹/₄ tsp salt

vegetable oil
2 bunches (3¹/₂ oz) *mitsuba* (trefoil)
pinch salt
4 sheets *nori* seaweed, toasted

小だいの棒ずし

1人分 430 kcal

◆材　料 (4人分)

すし飯 (→74頁)　800 g
小だいの笹漬け (市販品)
　4尾分 (150 g)
木の芽 (みじん切り)
　大さじ2
手酢 (水200 ccに酢大さじ1
　の割合)

◆作り方

1　小だいの笹漬けは身の厚い部分に切り込みを入れ、身の厚さを均等に開く。

2　手酢に浸した布巾をかたく絞って広げ、2尾の小だいの皮目を下に尾を合わせておき、すき間をへいだ身で埋めて長方形になるようにおく。→❶

3　すし飯に木の芽を混ぜ、2等分する。

4　手に手酢をつけて、しっかり握り、小だいの長さの棒状にまとめる。→❷

5　小だいにすし飯をのせて形を整え、手前の布巾をかぶせ、押さえてなじませる。くるりと向こうに返して、小だいを上にし、余った布巾を向こう側に引っ張ってぎゅっとしめる。巻き簀をかぶせて上から四角く角をつけるようにしっかり押さえる。両端の口を手で押さえて形を整える。→❸❹❺

6　食べやすい大きさに切り分ける。

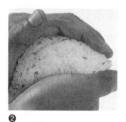
❶

❷

❸

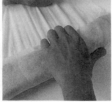
❹

❺

Sea Bream Sushi Logs

Kodai no Bō-zushi

430 kcal per serving

◆ DIRECTIONS

1 Butterfly cut the vinegared sea breams by slicing into the thick part, and trim meat to make them evenly thick.

2 Wet a cheesecloth with hand vinegar, wring tightly, and spread it out. Lay out 2 sea bream pieces, skin side down and with both tail sides next to one another. Use the trimmed meat to fill any slits, making a rectangular shape.→❶

3 Mix *kinome* sprigs with sushi rice, and divide into 2 portions.

4 Moisten your hands with hand vinegar, and form rice into bars to match the length of the laid out sea bream.→❷

5 Place bar of rice across the fish, and shape up. Bring up bottom flap of cheesecloth to cover rice and fish, and press lightly to secure. Roll the bar up so that the fish side comes out on top, and pull the rest of the cloth up from the other side to tighten. Cover with a bamboo rolling mat, and press to shape, making a square bar. Press both ends by hand to shape.→❸❹❺

6 Cut into pieces to serve.

◆ INGREDIENTS (4 servings)

28 oz sushi rice (→p. 75)

4 (5 1/4 oz) small vinegared sea bream, store-bought

2 Tbsp *kinome* sprigs, finely chopped

hand vinegar (1 Tbsp vinegar to 6 2/3 oz water)

ほうれん草のごまあえ

1人分 90 kcal

◆材　料(4人分)

ほうれん草　1束 (200 g)
塩　少々
ごまだれ
- 白ごま　大さじ4
- 砂糖　大さじ1
- しょうゆ　大さじ3
- だし　50 cc

◆作り方

1　ほうれん草は根元をよく洗い、
塩を加えたたっぷりの熱湯で、
多少歯ごたえが残るかたさにゆでる。
すぐに冷水にとり、10分ほどさらす。→❶❷

2　ごまだれを作る。ごまを弱火で
キツネ色になるまでいり、すり鉢で粒が
半分つぶれる状態にまですりつぶす。
調味料とだしを加えて混ぜ合わせる。→❸❹

3　ほうれん草の水けをしっかり絞り、
3cm長さに切る。

4　ほうれん草をごまだれであえる。

❶

❷

Spinach with Sesame Dressing

Hōrensō no Goma-ae

90 kcal per serving

◆ DIRECTIONS

1 Wash spinach thoroughly, especially the stems, and parboil in ample, lightly salted water until just tender.
Then rinse in cold water, and let soak for 10 minutes. →❶❷

2 To make sesame dressing, toast sesame seeds over low heat until brown, and grind in a mortar until the seeds are half-ground. Add the seasonings and *dashi*, and mix. →❸❹

3 Squeeze water from spinach, and cut into 1-inch lengths.

4 Dress spinach with sesame dressing.

◆ INGREDIENTS (4 servings)

1 bunch (7 oz) spinach
pinch salt
Sesame Dressing
⎰ 4 Tbsp white sesame
⎪   seeds
⎨ 1 Tbsp sugar
⎪ 3 Tbsp soy sauce
⎩ 1²/₃ oz *dashi*

❸

❹

クレソンのお浸し

1人分 60 kcal

◆**材 料**(4人分)

クレソン　4束 (200 g)
塩　少々
浸し地
    だし　400 cc
    みりん　大さじ3
    薄口しょうゆ　大さじ3
    塩　小さじ¼
松の実 (ロースト)　小さじ2

◆**作り方**

1　鍋に浸し地の材料を合わせ、
一煮立ちさせ、さます。

2　クレソンはたっぷりの湯で塩ゆでする。
すぐに水にさらし、水けを絞って
3cm長さに切る。

3　浸し地にクレソンを30分浸して、
味を含ませる。

4　器に盛りつけ、松の実を散らす。

応用
• 松の実の代わりに、白ごま、アーモンド、
ピーナッツなどでもよい。

Marinated Watercress
Kureson no Ohitashi

60 kcal per serving

◆ DIRECTIONS

1   Combine sauce ingredients in a saucepan, bring to a boil, and set aside to cool.

2   Parboil watercress in ample, lightly salted water. When it becomes tender, rinse in cold water and drain. Squeeze out excess water, and cut into 1-inch lengths.

3   Marinate watercress in sauce for 30 minutes to distribute flavor.

4   Serve in small bowls with a sprinkle of pine nuts on top.

NOTE
• White sesame seeds, almonds, or peanuts can also be used instead of pine nuts.

◆ INGREDIENTS (4 servings)

4 bunches (7 oz) watercress
pinch salt
Sauce
  1 2/3 U.S. cups *dashi*
  3 Tbsp *mirin*
  3 Tbsp light soy sauce
  1/4 tsp salt
2 tsp toasted pine nuts

かに酢

1人分 60 kcal

◆材　料(4人分)

わたりがに (がざみ)
　1杯 (400 g)
塩　適量
きゅうり　2本 (240 g)
しょうが酢
┌ だし　150 cc
│ 砂糖　大さじ2
│ 酢　大さじ6
│ 薄口しょうゆ　大さじ2
└ しょうがの絞り汁　大さじ1

◆作り方

1　かには塩を加えたたっぷりの熱湯で約20〜30分ゆでる。ざるに上げ、さめたら、身を取り出す。

2　きゅうりは縦半分に切り、種をスプーンなどでかき取る。小口から薄切りにする。ボールに入れて少量の塩をふり、5分おき、余分な水分を絞る。

3　しょうが酢を作る。鍋にだし、砂糖、酢、薄口しょうゆを入れ、一煮立ちさせ火をとめる。さめたらしょうがの絞り汁を加える。

4　かにときゅうりを盛り、しょうが酢をかける。

Vinegared Crab and Cucumber

Kani-su

60 kcal per serving

◆ DIRECTIONS

1 Boil crab in ample, lightly salted water for 20–30 minutes. Transfer crab to a sieve, and remove meat from shell when cool.

2 Cut cucumbers in half lengthwise, remove seeds with a spoon, and cut into thin slices. Place cucumbers in a bowl, sprinkle with salt, and let stand for 5 minutes. Wring out excess moisture.

3 To make ginger-vinegar dressing, combine *dashi*, sugar, vinegar and light soy sauce in a saucepan, bring to a boil, and remove from heat. When cooled, add fresh ginger juice.

4 Arrange crabmeat and cucumber on small plates, and pour dressing over.

◆ INGREDIENTS (4 servings)

1 (14 oz) fresh swimming crab (*gazami*-crab) in shell
salt
2 (8 1/2 oz) cucumbers
Ginger-Vinegar Dressing
5 oz *dashi*
2 Tbsp sugar
6 Tbsp rice vinegar
2 Tbsp light soy sauce
1 Tbsp fresh ginger juice

焼きしいたけポン酢あえ

1人分 10 kcal

◆材　料 (4人分)

生しいたけ　20枚 (400 g)
塩　適量
ポン酢 (市販品でも可)
　┌ 柑橘類の絞り汁　大さじ1
　└ しょうゆ　大さじ3
糸花がつお　適量

◆作り方

1　生しいたけの軸をのぞき、汚れを
ふき取って、塩をふる。

2　焼き網にのせ、中火で両面をまんべん
なく焼く。

3　熱い間に適当にさいて盛りつけ、
ポン酢をかけ、糸花がつおをのせる。

Grilled Mushrooms with Lemon-Soy Sauce

Yaki-Shiitake Ponzu-ae

10 kcal per serving

◆ DIRECTIONS

1 Remove stems of *shiitake* mushrooms, wipe dust off caps, and sprinkle with salt.

2 Place mushrooms on a cooking grill, and grill both sides over medium heat until done.

3 Tear mushrooms into pieces along grain while hot, and arrange in serving bowls. Add lemon-soy sauce (or *ponzu*), and top with bonito threads.

◆ INGREDIENTS (4 servings)

20 (14 oz) fresh *shiitake* mushrooms

salt

Lemon-Soy Sauce (or *Ponzu*)

⎰ 1 Tbsp lemon juice
⎱ 3 Tbsp soy sauce

bonito threads

サーモンとたこのマリネ

1人分　530 kcal

◆材　料 (4人分)

スモークサーモン　200 g
たこの足 (ゆでたもの)
　2本 (200 g)
いか (上身)　150 g
黒オリーブ　8個
ピーマン (赤、黄)　各¼個
わさびドレッシング
　白ワイン酢　大さじ2
　オリーブ油　150 cc
　しょうゆ　大さじ2
　おろしわさび (→116頁)
　　小さじ1
　塩、こしょう　各適量
パセリ (みじん切り)　大さじ1

◆作り方

1　サーモン、たこは一口大の斜め薄切り
にする。

2　いかは、表面に縦横の切り込みを入れ、
斜め薄切りにしてさっとゆでる。→❶❷

3　オリーブは薄く輪切りにする。

4　ピーマンは表面を焼いて皮をむき、
3mm幅の細切りにする。

5　ドレッシングの材料をビーターでよく
混ぜ合わせる。

6　ボールにサーモン、たこ、いか、
オリーブ、ピーマンを入れ、ドレッシングを
かける。

7　器に盛り、パセリを散らす。

❶

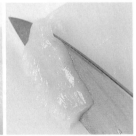
❷

Marinated Salmon and Octopus

Sāmon to Tako no Marine

530 kcal per serving

◆ DIRECTIONS

1 Slice salmon and octopus diagonally into thin bite-sized pieces.

2 Score each side of squid in a shallow diamond pattern, cut into thin slices diagonally, and parboil briefly. →❶❷

3 Slice olives into thin rings.

4 Grill bell peppers until skin turns black, peel, and cut peeled peppers into 1/8-inch thin strips.

5 Combine dressing ingredients in a bowl, and mix well with a whisk.

6 Place salmon, octopus, squid, olives, and bell peppers in a bowl, and dress with *wasabi* dressing.

7 Arrange in serving bowls, and sprinkle with chopped parsley.

◆ INGREDIENTS (4 servings)

7 oz smoked salmon

2 (7 oz) octopus tentacles, boiled

5 1/4 oz squid (body only)

8 black olives, seeded

1/4 red bell pepper

1/4 yellow bell pepper

Wasabi Dressing

  2 Tbsp white wine vinegar

  5 oz olive oil

  2 Tbsp soy sauce

  1 tsp grated *wasabi* horseradish (→p. 117)

  salt and pepper

1 Tbsp finely chopped parsley

牛肉サラダ

1人分 430 kcal

◆材　料 (4人分)

牛ロース肉 (薄切り)　400 g
わかめ (乾燥)　5 g
きゅうり　½本 (60 g)
にんじん　50 g
大根　100 g
長ねぎ　3 cm
プチトマト　4個
ごまだれ
　白いりごま　大さじ6
　砂糖　大さじ1
　みりん　大さじ1
　しょうゆ　大さじ5
　酢　大さじ7
　だし　100 cc

◆作り方

1　牛肉は2〜3等分に切る。熱湯にさっと
くぐらせ、すぐに水にとり、水けをきる。

2　わかめは水につけてもどし、水けを
絞り、3cm幅に切る。

3　きゅうり、大根、にんじん、長ねぎは
3cm長さのせん切りにし、混ぜ合わせ、
氷水につけてシャキッとさせ、水けをきる。

4　トマトは四つ割りにする。

5　ごまだれを作る。白いりごまをすり鉢
ですり、調味料を加えて混ぜ合わせる。
→❶

6　皿にせん切り野菜を敷き、わかめ、
肉をのせて、トマトを散らす。ごまだれを
添える。

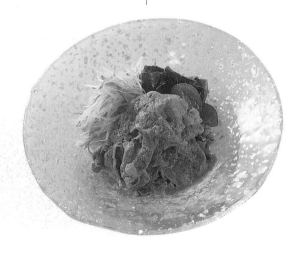

Beef Salad

Gyūniku Sarada

430 kcal per serving

◆ DIRECTIONS

1　Cut beef into 2–3 pieces. Blanch the beef very briefly in boiling water, transfer to a bowl of cold water immediately, drain, and pat dry.

2　Soak *wakame* seaweed in water, wring, and cut into 1-inch strips.

3　Julienne cucumber, *daikon* radish, carrot, and Japanese leek into 1-inch pieces, and combine. Soak in ice water to crisp, and drain.

4　Cut tomatoes into quarters.

5　To make sesame dressing, grind toasted white sesame seeds in a mortar, add seasonings, and mix well. →❶

6　Spread sliced vegetables on plates, arrange *wakame* and beef on top, and garnish with tomatoes. Serve with sesame dressing on the side.

◆ INGREDIENTS (4 servings)

14 oz beef sirloin, thinly sliced
1/6 oz dried *wakame* seaweed
1/2 (2 oz) cucumber
13/4 oz carrot
31/2 oz *daikon* radish
1-inch Japanese leek
4 cherry tomatoes
Sesame Dressing
　6 Tbsp toasted white sesame seeds
　1 Tbsp sugar
　1 Tbsp *mirin*
　5 Tbsp soy sauce
　7 Tbsp rice vinegar
　31/3 oz *dashi*

❶

鶏南蛮漬け

1人分 310 kcal

◆材　料 (4人分)

鶏もも肉 (骨なし)
　　1枚 (400 g)

南蛮酢

　だし　200 cc
　酢　200 cc
　砂糖　大さじ2
　みりん　大さじ3
　しょうゆ　大さじ4
　赤唐がらし (乾燥)　1本
　長ねぎ　1本
　玉ねぎ　1/4個
　レモンスライス　1枚

塩、こしょう　各適量

小麦粉　適量

揚げ油　適量

◆作り方

1　長ねぎは3cm長さに切り、フライパンで
さっと焼く。

2　玉ねぎは薄切りに、赤唐がらしは
小口切りにする。

3　南蛮酢を作る。鍋にだし、調味料を
入れて煮立て、長ねぎ、玉ねぎ、
赤唐がらし、レモンスライスを加えて火を
とめる。

4　鶏肉は3cm角に切り、塩、こしょうを
ふる。

5　鶏肉に小麦粉を薄くまぶし、揚げ油を
170℃に熱して、こんがり揚げる。

6　南蛮酢に揚げたての鶏肉を6時間
つけ込む。

Chicken Escabeche, *Nanban*-style

Tori Nanban-zuke

310 kcal per serving

◆ DIRECTIONS

1 Cut Japanese leek into 1-inch lengths, and sauté in a frying pan briefly.

2 Slice onion thinly, chop red chili pepper into fine rings.

3 To make marinade, place *dashi* and seasonings in a saucepan, bring to a boil, add leek, onion, red chili pepper and lemon, and remove from heat.

4 Cut chicken into 1-inch cubes, and sprinkle with salt and pepper.

5 Dust chicken lightly with flour. Preheat oil to 340°F, and deep-fry.

6 Marinate hot chicken in *Nanban* marinade for 6 hours.

◆ INGREDIENTS (4 servings)

14 oz chicken thighs, boned

Nanban Marinade

- 6²/₃ oz *dashi*
- 6²/₃ oz vinegar
- 2 Tbsp sugar
- 3 Tbsp *mirin*
- 4 Tbsp soy sauce
- 1 red chili pepper, dried
- 1 Japanese leek
- ¹/₄ onion
- 1 slice lemon

salt and pepper

flour

oil for deep-frying

オクラと長芋の
わさびじょうゆあえ

1人分 50 kcal

◆材　料(4人分)

オクラ　20本 (250 g)
塩　適量
長芋　100 g
わさびじょうゆ
  ┌ おろしわさび (→116頁)
  │　大さじ1
  └ しょうゆ　大さじ4
焼きのり　¼枚

◆作り方

1　オクラはへたを切り落とし、塩もみして、たっぷりの熱湯で塩ゆでにする。
ざるに上げてさまし、縦半分に切って種を除き、刻む。

2　長芋は皮をむき、3cm長さの細切りにする。

3　おろしわさびとしょうゆを混ぜ合わせ、わさびじょうゆを作る。

4　のりは細切りにする。→❶

5　器に長芋を敷き、オクラをのせる。
わさびじょうゆをかけ、のりを散らす。

❶

Okra and Mountain Yams with *Wasabi* Sauce

Okura to Nagaimo no Wasabi-jōyu-ae

50 kcal per serving

◆ DIRECTIONS

1 Remove stems from okra, rub with salt, and parboil in ample hot water. Drain in a sieve, and let cool. Cut in half lengthwise, remove seeds, and chop finely.

2 Peel mountain yam, and julienne into 1-inch lengths.

3 Combine grated *wasabi* and soy sauce.

4 Cut *nori* seaweed into thin strips. →❶

5 Distribute mountain yam evenly in serving bowls, and mound okra on top. Pour *wasabi* sauce over, and garnish with *nori* seaweed.

◆ INGREDIENTS (4 servings)

20 pods (9 oz) okra
salt
3 1/2 oz mountain yam
Wasabi-Soy Sauce
 [1 Tbsp grated *wasabi*
    horseradish (→p. 117)
   4 Tbsp soy sauce
1/4 sheet *nori* seaweed,
  toasted

えびとリークの
からし酢みそあえ

1人分 150 kcal

◆材　料(4人分)

えび (30 gの生きたもの)
　4尾
塩　適量
ポロねぎ (＝西洋ねぎ＝リーク)
　1本 (200 g)
からし酢みそ
┌白みそ　大さじ5
│卵黄　1個
│砂糖　大さじ3
┤酢　大さじ2
│薄口しょうゆ　大さじ1
│練りがらし　小さじ1
└だし　大さじ2
タラゴン (あれば)

◆作り方

1　えびは頭と背わたを取り、腹を上にして頭から尾に向けて串を刺し、約3分塩ゆでする。水に取り、さめたら串を抜き、殻をむいて2等分にする。→❶

2　ポロねぎは根の方に十文字の切り込みを入れて、たっぷりの湯でゆでる。水にさらし、さめたら1cm幅に切る。

3　からし酢みそを作る。白みそと卵黄をよく混ぜ、調味料、だしの順に加え混ぜ合わせる。裏ごしして、きめを細かくする。→❷

4　器にからし酢みそを敷き、えび、ポロねぎを盛り、タラゴンをのせる。

❶

❷

Shrimp and Leeks with Mustard-Miso Sauce

Ebi to Riku no Karashi-sumiso-ae

150 kcal per serving

◆ DIRECTIONS

1 Devein shrimp and remove heads. Hold shrimp with underside up and skewer lengthwise, starting from the head end. Parboil shrimp in salted water for 3 minutes. Soak in cold water, and when cool, remove skewers. Shell shrimp and cut each into 2 pieces. →❶

2 Score a cross on root end of leek, and parboil in ample hot water. Soak in cold water, and cut into ⅜-inch lengths when cool.

3 To make mustard-miso sauce, mix white miso and egg yolk well, add seasonings, *dashi*, and mix. Strain sauce through a sieve. →❷

4 Spread sauce on serving plates, arrange shrimp and leek on top, and garnish with tarragon.

◆ INGREDIENTS (4 servings)

4 fresh shrimp, 1 oz each
salt
1 (7 oz) leek
Mustard-Miso Sauce
  5 Tbsp white miso
  1 egg yolk
  3 Tbsp sugar
  2 Tbsp vinegar
  1 Tbsp light soy sauce
  1 tsp yellow mustard
  2 Tbsp *dashi*
tarragon (optional)

ゆで鶏とグレープフルーツの アーモンドあえ

1人分 280 kcal

◆材 料（4人分）

鶏胸肉（皮なし） 120 g
塩 少々
グレープフルーツ 1個
コーンサラダ（＝マーシュ）
　60 g
アーモンドソース
　┌ アーモンド（皮つき） 100 g
　│ 砂糖 大さじ2
　│ みりん 大さじ1
　│ 酢 大さじ5
　│ しょうゆ 大さじ3
　└ だし 100 cc

◆作り方

1 鶏肉はたっぷりの湯に塩を加えて
弱火で15分ゆでる。そのままさまし、
さめたら手で細くさく。

2 グレープフルーツは果肉を取り出し、
2等分にする。

3 コーンサラダは1枚ずつ丁寧に
水洗いして、水けをきる。

4 アーモンドは熱湯でゆで、薄皮を除き、
から鍋で香ばしくなるまでいる。

5 すり鉢に入れてよくすりつぶし、
調味料を加えて混ぜ合わせ、だしで
のばす。→❶

6 器にアーモンドソースを敷き、鶏肉、
グレープフルーツ、コーンサラダを盛る。

Chicken with Grapefruit in Almond Sauce

Yudedori to Gurēpu-furūtsu no Āmondo-ae

280 kcal per serving

◆ DIRECTIONS

1   Gently boil chicken in ample, lightly salted water for 15 minutes over low heat. Let it stand to cool, and tear chicken into thin strips by hand.

2   Seed grapefruit sections, remove section skin, and slice each section in half lengthwise.

3   Rinse each corn salad leaf carefully, and drain well.

4   Soak almonds in hot water, discard thin skin, and toast in a dry frying pan until golden brown.

5   Grind the almonds in a mortar (or food proccessor), add seasonings and *dashi*, and mix well to make almond sauce. →❶

6   Spread almond sauce on serving plates, and arrange chicken, grapefruit, and corn salad on top.

◆ INGREDIENTS (4 servings)

4 1/5 oz chicken breast, skinned
pinch salt
1 grapefruit
2 oz corn salad (*mâche*)
Almond Sauce
   3 1/2 oz shelled almonds with skin
   2 Tbsp sugar
   1 Tbsp *mirin*
   5 Tbsp vinegar
   3 Tbsp soy sauce
   3 1/3 oz *dashi*

❶

かにとアボカドの黄身酢あえ

1人分 260 kcal

◆材 料(4人分)

かに (缶詰) 100g

アボカド 1個

アンディーブ (=ベルギーチコリ)
　8枚

イクラ 適量

黄身酢
　卵黄 3個
　酢 大さじ2
　みりん 大さじ1
　砂糖 大さじ1
　薄口しょうゆ 小さじ1
　塩 少々
　だし 大さじ3

チャービル 適量

◆作り方

1 かにには軟骨を取り除き、汁けをきる。

2 アボカドは縦半分に切って、種を取り、皮をむき、5mm角に切る。アンディーブは1枚ずつ丁寧に洗う。

3 イクラはぬるま湯でさっと洗い、水けをきる。

4 鍋に黄身酢の材料を合わせ、湯せんにして、かき混ぜながら約10分練る。裏ごしして、きめを細かくする。→❶

5 ボールにかにとアボカドを入れて、黄身酢であえる。

6 アンディーブにのせて、イクラを散らし、器に盛ってチャービルを添える。

❶

Crab and Avocado
with Golden Yolk Sauce

Kani to Abokado no Kimizu-ae

260 kcal per serving

◆ DIRECTIONS

1   Remove any cartilage and shell from crabmeat, and drain.

2   Cut avocado in half lengthwise, remove seed and skin, and cut into ⅛-inch cubes. Rinse each endive leaf carefully, and drain well.

3   Rinse salmon roe in lukewarm water, and drain.

4   Combine all ingredients for golden yolk sauce in a saucepan, place the pan in a bowl of hot water over heat, and keep stirring for 10 minutes until thick. Strain the sauce through a sieve. →❶

5   Combine crabmeat and avocado in a bowl, and mix with golden yolk sauce.

6   Spoon the mixture onto each endive leaf, sprinkle with salmon roe, and garnish with chervil.

◆ INGREDIENTS (4 servings)

3 ½ oz canned crabmeat
1 avocado
8 endive leaves
salmon roe
Golden Yolk Sauce
  3 egg yolks
  2 Tbsp vinegar
  1 Tbsp *mirin*
  1 Tbsp sugar
  1 tsp light soy sauce
  pinch salt
  3 Tbsp *dashi*
chervil

和風ピクルス

1人分 60 kcal

◆材　料(4人分)

きゅうり　2本(240 g)
にんじん　1本(150 g)
セロリ　1本(100 g)
塩　適量
漬け汁
　ワイン酢　200 cc
　水　200 cc
　グラニュー糖　大さじ2
　塩　大さじ1
　昆布　5 cm
赤唐がらし(乾燥)　2本

◆作り方

1　きゅうりは塩をまぶし、まな板の上で
ゴロゴロころがして、水で洗い、5cm長さ
に切る。にんじん、セロリは1cm角5cm長さ
の棒状にする。

2　塩水(水600ccに塩大さじ1の割合)
に2時間つける。

3　鍋に漬け汁の材料を入れて火にかけ、
沸騰寸前に昆布を取り出し、煮立てる。

4　きゅうり、にんじん、セロリの水けを
ふき取り、ふたつきの容器(保存瓶)に詰
め、赤唐がらしを加えて、熱々の漬け汁を
注ぎ、ふたをする。→❶

5　さめたら、冷蔵庫で1晩以上つける。
1週間はもつ。

Pickled Vegetables, Japanese-style

Wafū Pikurusu

60 kcal per serving

◆ DIRECTIONS

1 Salt cucumbers and roll them, pressing lightly, on a cutting board. Rinse with water, and cut into 2-inch lengths. Cut carrot and celery into 3/8 × 3/8 × 2-inch sticks.

2 Soak vegetables in salted water (1 Tbsp salt to 2 1/2 U.S. cups water) for 2 hours.

3 Heat pickling juice ingredients in a saucepan and bring to a boil, removing *konbu* kelp just before boiling.

4 Drain and pat dry vegetables, transfer to a pickling jar, and add red chili peppers. Fill jar with hot pickling juice, and seal. →❶

5 When cooled, place in a refrigerator, and let stand at least overnight. The pickles stay fresh for 1 week.

◆ INGREDIENTS (4 servings)

2 (8 1/2 oz) cucumbers
1 (5 1/4 oz) carrot
1 (3 1/2 oz) stalk celery
salt
Pickling Juice
  6 2/3 oz wine vinegar
  6 2/3 oz water
  2 Tbsp granulated sugar
  1 Tbsp salt
  2-inch square *konbu* kelp
2 red chili peppers, dried

❶

甘酢漬け 2種

菊花かぶ甘酢漬け

1人分 20 kcal

◆材　料 (4人分)

小かぶ　1個 (100 g)
塩　適量
甘酢
　[酢　大さじ4
　　水　大さじ4
　　砂糖　小さじ2
赤唐がらし (小口切り)　1本

◆作り方

1　かぶは皮をむき、2cm厚さの輪切りにして、上から⅔ぐらいまで縦横に細かく切り込みを入れる。裏返して底の方から2cm角に切る。→❶

2　塩水 (水400ccに塩大さじ1の割合) に15分つけてしんなりさせる。

3　甘酢の材料を混ぜ合わせる。

4　かぶの水けを絞って、甘酢に赤唐がらしを加えたものに1時間つける。

5　かぶを軽く絞って、菊の花のように形づくり、赤唐がらしの小口切りを中央に飾る。

しょうがの甘酢漬け

1人分 30 kcal

◆材　料 (4人分)

しょうが　50 g
塩　適量
甘酢
　[酢　大さじ4
　　水　大さじ4
　　砂糖　小さじ2

◆作り方

1　しょうがは皮をむき、ごく薄く切る。さっと熱湯に通し、ざるに広げて入れ、軽く塩をふる。

2　さめたら甘酢に1時間以上つける。

Sweet-Vinegared Pickles
Amazu-zuke

Chrysanthemum Turnip
Kikka-kabu Amazu-zuke

20 kcal per serving

◆ DIRECTIONS

1 Peel turnip, and cut horizontally into ¾-inch-thick rounds. Score the rounds, then turn 90° and score again to make a fine grid penetrating ⅔ through. Turn rounds over, and cut into ¾-inch cubes. →❶

2 Soak turnip cubes in salted water (1 Tbsp salt to 1⅔ U.S. cups water) for 15 minutes to make them tender.

3 Combine sweet vinegar ingredients, and mix well.

4 Wring out excess moisture from turnip, and soak in sweet vinegar with red chili pepper for 1 hour.

5 Wring turnip lightly and spread out the "petals" of chrysanthemum turnip. Garnish each flower with a thin ring of red chili pepper in the center.

◆ INGREDIENTS (4 servings)

1 (3½ oz) turnip
salt
Sweet Vinegar
  ⎧ 4 Tbsp vinegar
  ⎨ 4 Tbsp water
  ⎩ 2 tsp sugar
1 red chili pepper, chopped into thin rings

Sweet-Vinegared Ginger
Shōga no Amazu-zuke

30 kcal per serving

◆ DIRECTIONS

1 To make sweet-vinegared ginger, peel ginger and slice very thinly. Blanch in boiling water, drain in a sieve, and sprinkle lightly with salt.

2 When cool, soak in sweet vinegar at least 1 hour.

◆ INGREDIENTS (4 servings)

1¾ oz fresh ginger
salt
Sweet Vinegar
  ⎧ 4 Tbsp vinegar
  ⎨ 4 Tbsp water
  ⎩ 2 tsp sugar

まぐろのおろし造り

1人分 150 kcal

◆材 料(4人分)

まぐろ 400 g
大根 200 g
青ねぎ 2本
焼きのり ½枚
しょうゆ 適量
わさび 適量

◆作り方

1 まぐろは2cm角に切る。

2 大根は皮をむき、おろして、軽く絞って余分な汁をきる。
わさびもおろしておく*(市販品の粉わさび、冷凍おろしわさびでもよい)。

3 青ねぎは小口から刻み、水にさらして、水けを絞る。

4 のりは、細かくちぎる。

5 大根おろし、ねぎ、のりを混ぜ合わせる。

6 器にまぐろを盛り、5を添えて、わさびをのせ、周囲にしょうゆをはる。

*わさびのおろし方:茎を切り落とし、切り口のほうから、必要な分だけの皮を削って、目の細かいおろし金で輪を描きながらおろす。→❶❷

❶

❷

Tuna Sashimi with Grated Radish

Maguro no Oroshi-zukuri

150 kcal per serving

◆ DIRECTIONS

1 Cut tuna into ¾-inch cubes.

2 Peel *daikon* radish, grate, and squeeze lightly to remove excess moisture.
Grate *wasabi*.* (Powdered, tubed, or frozen *wasabi* is also available.)

3 Chop scallions finely, rinse in cold water, and wring.

4 Crumble *nori* seaweed into small pieces.

5 Combine grated *daikon*, scallions, and *nori* seaweed, and mix.

6 Place tuna cubes in dishes, mound the *daikon* mixture next to the tuna, top the mound with *wasabi* horseradish, and pour soy sauce around the tuna.

* To grate *wasabi* horseradish: Discard stem, peel from the top end only for as much as you need, and grate finely in a circular motion. →❶❷

◆ INGREDIENTS (4 servings)

14 oz fresh tuna fillet

7 oz *daikon* radish

2 scallions

½ sheet *nori* seaweed, toasted

soy sauce

wasabi horseradish

たいの薄造り
中華風ドレッシング

1人分 180 kcal

◆材 料(4人分)

たい (皮なし、上身) 400 g
長ねぎ 5 cm
青じそ 4枚
ピーナッツ (ロースト)
　大さじ1
中華風ドレッシング
[砂糖 小さじ1
　酢 大さじ2
　酒 大さじ1
　しょうゆ 50 cc
　ごま油 小さじ2

◆作り方

1 たいは薄くそぎ切りにして、切ったものから順に少しずつ重ねながら器に並べて盛りつける。→❶

2 長ねぎは縦に切り込みを入れ、芯を取って細いせん切りにし、水にさらして、水けをきる。→❷

3 青じそはせん切りにし、水にさらして水けをきる。

4 ピーナッツは刻む。

5 ドレッシングの材料を混ぜ合わせる。

6 たいにかけ、ねぎと青じそをのせ、ピーナッツを散らす。

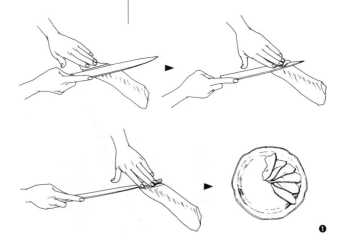

❶

Sea Bream Sashimi with Chinese Dressing

Tai no Usu-zukuri, Chūka-fū doresshingu

180 kcal per serving

◆ DIRECTIONS

1 Cut or shave the fillet into thin slices. Transfer each slice to a plate overlapping them slightly to make a rosette. →❶

2 Slit leek lengthwise, remove the core, and cut into fine julienne strips, soak in cold water. Drain. →❷

3 Cut *shiso* leaves into thin strips, soak in cold water. Drain.

4 Chop peanuts.

5 Combine Chinese dressing ingredients, and mix well.

6 Pour dressing over sea bream, top with Japanese leek and *shiso* leaves, and sprinkle with peanuts.

◆ INGREDIENTS (4 servings)

14 oz sea bream fillet
2-inch Japanese leek
4 green *shiso* leaves
1 Tbsp roasted peanuts
Chinese Dressing
   1 tsp sugar
   2 Tbsp rice vinegar
   1 Tbsp *saké*
   1²/₃ oz soy sauce
   2 tsp sesame oil

❷

牛肉のたたき

1人分 230 kcal

◆材　料(4人分)

牛ヒレ肉　400 g
塩、こしょう　各少々
サラダ油　適量
薬味
- おろししょうが　大さじ2
- 大根おろし　大さじ4
- 一味唐がらし　少々
- 青ねぎ　4本
- みょうが　4本
- 青じそ　8枚
ポン酢 (市販品でも可)
- 柑橘類の絞り汁　大さじ3
- しょうゆ　100 cc

◆作り方

1　牛肉は全体に塩、こしょうをする。フライパンに油を熱し、両面を好みの焼きかげんに焼く。氷水につけて、あら熱を取り、水けをふき取る。

2　大根おろしと一味唐がらしを混ぜ合わせる。

3　青ねぎは小口から刻み、水にさらして、水けをきる。

4　みょうが、青じそはせん切りにして、水にさらして、水けをきる。

5　ポン酢の材料を合わせる。

6　牛肉を3mm厚さの薄切りにして皿に並べ、薬味、ポン酢を添える。

Quick-Seared Beef

Gyūniku no Tataki

230 kcal per serving

◆ DIRECTIONS

1 Sprinkle beef with salt and pepper. Heat a lightly oiled frying pan, cook the meat briefly until the outside is slightly singed. Remove from heat, plunge into ice water, and pat dry.

2 Mix grated *daikon* and chili pepper flakes.

3 Chop scallions finely, rinse in cold water, and drain.

4 Cut *myoga* and *shiso* leaves into fine slivers, soak in cold water, and drain.

5 Mix lemon-soy sauce ingredients.

6 Slice beef very thinly (⅛-inch), and arrange meat and condiments on a dish. Serve with dipping sauce.

◆ INGREDIENTS (4 servings)

14 oz beef tenderloin
salt and pepper
vegetable oil
Condiments
  2 Tbsp grated fresh ginger
  4 Tbsp grated *daikon* radish
  pinch chili pepper flakes
  4 scallions
  4 "buds" *myoga* ginger
  8 green *shiso* leaves
Lemon-Soy Sauce
  (or *Ponzu*)
  3 Tbsp lemon juice
  3⅓ oz soy sauce

シーフードサラダ造り

1人分 340 kcal

◆材　料(4人分)

すずき(皮なし、上身)
　　150 g
帆立て貝 (殻つき)　4個
えび (30 gの生きたもの)
　　8尾
ドレッシング
　　レモンの絞り汁　大さじ3
　　りんご酢　大さじ3
　　薄口しょうゆ　大さじ1
　　オリーブ油　100 cc
　　塩、こしょう　各適量
あさつき　5本

◆作り方

1　すずきは2〜3mm厚さのそぎ切りにする。→❶

2　帆立て貝は殻をあけ、貝柱を取り出し、2〜3枚に薄切りにする。→❷

3　えびは頭を取り、背わたもいっしょに引き抜く。熱湯でゆで、殻が赤くなったら、すぐに水にとり、殻をむき、2〜3等分に切る。→❸

4　ドレッシングの材料を混ぜ合わせる。

5　あさつきは小口から刻む。

6　器に盛りつけ、ドレッシングをかけて、あさつきを散らす。

❶

❷

❸

Seafood Salad

Shifūdo Sarada-zukuri

340 kcal per serving

◆ DIRECTIONS

1   Cut or shave the sea bass fillet into thin slices. → ❶

2   Open scallop shells, take out the core meat, cut into 2–3 thin slices. → ❷

3   Discard shrimp heads, deveining at the same time. Cook in boiling water, and as soon as shells turn red, plunge into cold water. Peel shrimp, and cut into 2–3 pieces. → ❸

4   Mix all dressing ingredients.

5   Chop *asatsuki* chives finely.

6   Arrange seafood on plates, add dressing, and sprinkle with *asatsuki* chives.

◆ INGREDIENTS (4 servings)

5 1/4 oz fresh sea bass fillet
4 scallops with shells
8 fresh shrimp, 1 oz each
Dressing
 ⌜ 3 Tbsp lemon juice
 │ 3 Tbsp apple vinegar
 ⟨ 1 Tbsp light soy sauce
 │ 3 1/3 oz olive oil
 ⌞ salt and pepper
5 *asatsuki*
 (Japanese chives)

すき焼き

1人分 860 kcal

◆材 料 (4人分)

牛ロース肉 (薄切り)
  600〜800 g
牛脂 適量
木綿豆腐 ½丁 (150 g)
糸こんにゃく 150 g
生しいたけ 8枚
長ねぎ 2本
三つ葉 2束 (100 g)
割り下
  酒 大さじ3
  水 100 cc
  しょうゆ 200 cc
  みりん 200 cc
  砂糖 大さじ6
卵 4個

◆作り方

1 鍋に割り下の材料を合わせて、一煮立ちさせる。

2 豆腐は一口大に切る。糸こんにゃくは食べやすい長さに切り、湯通しして、ざるに上げ、水けをきる。しいたけは軸を取り、2等分に、長ねぎは斜め切り、三つ葉は3cm長さに切る。大皿に盛り合わせる。

3 牛肉は別の皿に盛る。

4 すき焼き用の鉄鍋を熱し、牛脂を溶かして、肉を焼く。焼き色がついたら割り下をひたひた量注ぎ、好みの材料を少しずつ加えながら煮る。煮えたら溶き卵をつけて食べる。→❶❷

Sukiyaki

860 kcal per serving

◆ DIRECTIONS

1   Combine sauce ingredients in a saucepan, and bring to a boil.

2   Cut tofu into bite-sized pieces. Cut *ito-konnyaku* filaments into lengths that are easy to eat, blanch in boiling water briefly, and drain in a sieve. Trim stems from *shiitake*, and cut caps in half. Slice Japanese leeks diagonally. Cut *mitsuba* into 1-inch lengths. Arrange all these ingredients on a large plate.

3   Arrange beef on a separate plate.

4   Heat a sukiyaki skillet, grease it with beef suet, and sauté beef. When brown, pour sauce to cover beef almost completely, and gradually add all other ingredients. When food is cooked, take pieces from the skillet and eat, dipping into beaten eggs.→❶❷

◆ INGREDIENTS (4 servings)

21–28 oz beef loin, thinly sliced
beef suet
1/2 cake (5 1/4 oz) "cotton" tofu
5 1/4 oz *ito-konnyaku* (devil's tongue jelly filaments)
8 fresh *shiitake* mushrooms
2 Japanese leeks
2 bunches (3 1/2 oz) *mitsuba* (trefoil)
Sauce ("*Warishita*")
  ⎡ 3 Tbsp saké
  ⎢ 3 1/3 oz water
  ⎢ 6 2/3 oz soy sauce
  ⎢ 6 2/3 oz mirin
  ⎣ 6 Tbsp sugar
4 eggs

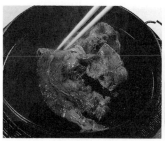

❶

❷

しゃぶしゃぶ

1人分 690 kcal

◆材 料(4人分)

牛ロース肉 (薄切り)
　600〜800 g
白菜　4枚 (200 g)
しめじ　1パック (150 g)
長ねぎ　2本
絹ごし豆腐　½丁 (150 g)
くず切り　1袋
昆布だし
　⎰ 水　2000 cc
　⎱ 昆布　50 g
ごまだれ
　⎧ 白いりごま　大さじ6
　⎪ だし　200 cc
　⎪ 酒 (煮きり)　大さじ5
　⎨ みりん (煮きり)　大さじ1
　⎪ 砂糖　小さじ1
　⎩ 薄口しょうゆ　大さじ3
ポン酢 (市販品でも可)
　⎧ 柑橘類の絞り汁　150 cc
　⎪ しょうゆ　150 cc
　⎨ 酒 (煮きり)　大さじ3
　⎩ みりん (煮きり)　大さじ1
薬味
　⎧ さらしねぎ (→32頁)
　⎪ 　大さじ4
　⎨ 大根おろし　大さじ8
　⎩ 一味唐がらし　適量

◆作り方

1　昆布は布巾でさっとふいて、汚れを
落とす。食卓に出せる鍋に分量の水と
昆布を入れ、3時間おく。

2　白菜の葉はざく切り、芯は細切りに
する。しめじは石づきを取って小分けに、
長ねぎは斜め切りにする。豆腐は
一口大に切り、くず切りは熱湯でもどし、
適当な長さに切って、水けをきる。
皿に盛り合わせ、肉は別皿に盛る。

3　ごまだれを作る。いりごまをすり鉢で
すり、調味料を混ぜ合わせ、器に入れる。

4　ポン酢、薬味を用意する。

5　1の鍋を火にかけ、沸騰直前に昆布を
取り出し、好みの材料を入れ、煮えたら
ごまだれか好みの薬味を入れた
ポン酢につけて食べる。

Shabu-Shabu

690 kcal per serving

◆ DIRECTIONS

1 Wipe *konbu* kelp lightly with cheesecloth to clean. Place water and *konbu* kelp in a large pot that is presentable for the table; let stand for 3 hours.

2 Cut Chinese cabbage leaves roughly into pieces, slice stalk parts thinly. Trim stems from *shimeji*, and tear into small clusters. Cut Japanese leeks diagonally, and tofu into bite-sized pieces. Soak *kuzukiri* noodles in hot water, drain, and cut to manageable lengths. Arrange these ingredients on a large plate, beef on a separate plate.

3 To make sesame sauce, grind toasted sesame seeds in a mortar, add seasonings, and transfer to a bowl.

4 Prepare lemon-soy sauce and condiments.

5 Place pot over heat, remove *konbu* just before boiling, and cook other ingredients as needed while eating, with either sesame sauce or lemon-soy sauce and condiments.

◆ INGREDIENTS (4 servings)

21–28 oz beef loin, thinly sliced
4 leaves (7 oz) Chinese cabbage
1 pack (5¼ oz) *shimeji* mushrooms
2 Japanese leeks
½ cake (5¼ oz) "silken" tofu
1 pack *kuzukiri* clear noodles

Konbu Kelp *Dashi*
⎰ 8⅓ U.S. cups water
⎱ 1¾ oz *konbu* kelp

Sesame Sauce
⎰ 6 Tbsp white sesame seeds, toasted
⎪ 6⅔ oz *dashi*
⎨ 5 Tbsp boiled *saké*
⎪ 1 Tbsp boiled *mirin*
⎪ 1 tsp sugar
⎱ 3 Tbsp light soy sauce

Lemon-Soy Sauce (or *Ponzu*)
⎰ 5 oz lemon juice
⎪ 5 oz soy sauce
⎨ 3 Tbsp boiled *saké*
⎱ 1 Tbsp boiled *mirin*

Condiments
⎰ 4 Tbsp rinsed scallions (→p. 33)
⎨ 8 Tbsp grated *daikon* radish
⎱ chili pepper flakes

寄せ鍋

1人分 350 kcal

◆材 料(4人分)

たい (上身、皮つき) 150 g
いか (上身) 100 g
えび (30 gの無頭) 8尾
はまぐり (50 gのもの) 4個
鶏もも肉 ½枚 (200 g)
木綿豆腐 ½丁 (150 g)
春雨 20 g
白菜 6枚 (300 g)
ほうれん草 1束 (200 g)
しめじ 1パック (150 g)
長ねぎ 2本
煮汁
 だし 2000 cc
 塩 小さじ2
 みりん 100 cc
 薄口しょうゆ 150 cc
薬味
 さらしねぎ (→32頁)
 おろししょうが
 大根おろし
 レモンのくし形切り
 一味唐がらし
 など適当に

◆作り方

1 たいは1cm幅に切る。いかは一口大に切る。えびは背わたを取り、熱湯でさっとゆでて殻をむく。はまぐりは塩水で洗う。鶏肉は3cm角に切り、熱湯にさっと通し、皿に盛り合わせる。

2 豆腐は3cm角に切り、春雨は水に15分つけてもどし、水けをきる。白菜、ほうれん草は別々に熱湯でゆで、ざるに上げてさます。巻き簀の上に白菜を広げ、ほうれん草を中心におき、かたく巻き、2cm幅に切る。しめじは石づきを取って小分けにする。長ねぎは斜め切りにする。皿に盛り合わせる。

3 薬味を用意する。

4 食卓に出せる鍋に煮汁を入れて火にかけ、好みの材料を加え、煮えたら好みの薬味で食べる。

Seafood and Chicken Pot

Yose-nabe

350 kcal per serving

◆ DIRECTIONS

1 Cut sea bream into ³⁄₈-inch wide strips, and squid into bite-sized pieces. Devein shrimp, parboil briefly, and shell. Wash clams with salted water. Cut chicken into 1-inch cubes, parboil briefly. Arrange ingredients on a large plate.

2 Cut tofu into 1-inch cubes. Soak *harusame* noodles in water for 15 minutes, and drain. Parboil Chinese cabbage and spinach separately, drain in a sieve, and cool. Lay cabbage leaves on a bamboo rolling mat, place spinach in the middle, and roll tight, then cut into ³⁄₄-inch wide pieces. Trim stems from *shimeji*, and tear into small clusters. Cut Japanese leeks diagonally. Arrange these ingredients on a large plate.

3 Prepare condiments.

4 Place stock in a presentable pot over heat, and add other ingredients while eating, with condiments to taste.

◆ INGREDIENTS (4 servings)

5¹⁄₄ oz sea bream fillet with skin

3¹⁄₂ oz squid (body only)

8 shrimp in shells without heads, 1 oz each

4 hard-shell clams, 1³⁄₄ oz each

¹⁄₂ (7 oz) boned chicken thigh

¹⁄₂ cake (5¹⁄₄ oz) "cotton" tofu

²⁄₃ oz harusame (saifun noodles)

6 leaves (10¹⁄₂ oz) Chinese cabbage

1 bunch (7 oz) spinach

1 pack (5¹⁄₄ oz) *shimeji* mushrooms

2 Japanese leeks

Stock
- 8¹⁄₃ U.S. cups *dashi*
- 2 tsp salt
- 3¹⁄₃ oz *mirin*
- 5 oz light soy sauce

Condiments
- rinsed scallions (→p. 33)
- grated fresh ginger
- grated *daikon* radish
- lemon wedges
- chili pepper flakes

おでん

| 1人分　420 kcal |

◆材　料 (4人分)

たこの足 (ゆでたもの)
　4本 (400 g)
大根 (2cm厚さの輪切り)
　4切れ
里芋　8個 (300 g)
こんにゃく　1枚 (200 g)
厚揚げ　2枚 (200 g)
ごぼう天　4本 (200 g)
煮汁
　だし　2000 cc
　酒　大さじ6
　砂糖　大さじ3
　みりん　大さじ5
　薄口しょうゆ　大さじ5
　しょうゆ　大さじ5
　干しえび　30 g
練りがらし　適量
薬味
　さらしねぎ (→32頁)
　ゆずの皮 (みじん切り)
　一味唐がらし
　　など適当に

◆作り方

1　たこの足は2等分に切る。

2　大根、里芋は皮をむき、水から
柔らかくなるまで下ゆでする。

3　こんにゃくは塩もみしてさっとゆで、
表面に斜めに縦横の切り込みを入れ、
8等分に切る。

4　厚揚げ、ごぼう天は熱湯に通して
油抜きする。厚揚げは2等分に切る。

5　鍋におでんの材料と煮汁を入れて、
弱火でじっくり2〜3時間煮込む。

6　好みで練りがらし、薬味をつけて
食べる。

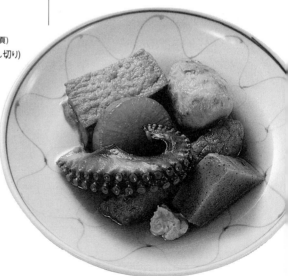

Oden Stew

Oden

420 kcal per serving

◆ DIRECTIONS

1 Cut octopus tentacles in half lengthwise.

2 Peel *daikon* radish and taros, and boil until tender.

3 Rub *konnyaku* with salt, parboil briefly, cut across the surfaces, making diagonal slits, and cut the cake into 8 pieces.

4 Douse deep-fried tofu and burdock fishcake rolls with boiling water to remove excess oil. Cut tofu in half.

5 Place all ingredients and stock in a pot, and cook over low heat for 2–3 hours.

6 Serve with mustard and condiments to taste.

◆ INGREDIENTS (4 servings)

4 (14 oz) octopus tentacles, boiled

4 slices *daikon* radish, 3/4-inch thick

8 (10 1/2 oz) taros

1 cake (7 oz) *konnyaku* (devil's tongue jelly)

2 cake (7 oz) "thick" deep-fried tofu (*atsuage*)

4 (7 oz) burdock fishcake rolls

Stock

- 8 1/3 U.S. cups *dashi*
- 6 Tbsp *saké*
- 3 Tbsp sugar
- 5 Tbsp *mirin*
- 5 Tbsp light soy sauce
- 5 Tbsp soy sauce
- 1 oz dried shrimp

yellow mustard

Condiments

- rinsed scallions (→p. 33)
- chopped *yuzu* citron rind
- chili pepper flakes

鶏の水炊き

1人分　570 kcal

◆材　料(4人分)

鶏もも肉 (骨つき)　1 kg
白菜　6枚 (300 g)
ほうれん草　1束 (200 g)
生しいたけ　8枚
長ねぎ　2本
もち　3 cm角 4個
昆布だし
- 水　2000 cc
- 昆布　50 g
ポン酢 (市販品でも可)
- 柑橘類の絞り汁　150 cc
- しょうゆ　150 cc
- 酒 (煮きり)　大さじ3
- みりん (煮きり)　大さじ1
薬味
- さらしねぎ (→32頁)
- 大根おろし
- 一味唐がらし
  - など適当に

◆作り方

1　昆布は布巾でさっとふいて、汚れを落とす。食卓に出せる鍋に分量の水と昆布を入れ、3時間おく。

2　鶏肉は一口大のぶつ切りにし、湯通しをし、水けをきって、皿に盛る。

3　白菜、ほうれん草はざく切りにする。しいたけは軸を取って四つ割りにする。長ねぎは斜め切りにする。もちは一口大に切り、こんがり焼く。皿に盛り合わせる。

4　ポン酢、薬味を用意する。

5　1の鍋を火にかけ、沸騰直前に昆布を取り出す。

6　好みの材料を入れ、煮えたら好みの薬味を入れたポン酢につけて食べる。

八寸

先付

Chicken Pot

Tori no Mizutaki

570 kcal per serving

◆ DIRECTIONS

1 Wipe *konbu* kelp lightly with cheesecloth to clean. Place water and *konbu* kelp in a large pot that is presentable for the table; let stand for 3 hours.

2 Cut chicken into bite-sized chunks, douse with hot water, drain, and arrange on a plate.

3 Cut Chinese cabbage and spinach roughly into pieces. Remove stems from *shiitake* mushrooms, and cut the caps into quarters. Slice Japanese leeks diagonally. Cut rice cakes into bite-sized pieces, broil until brown, and arrange on a plate.

4 Prepare lemon-soy sauce, and condiments.

5 Place the pot over heat, and remove *konbu* kelp just before boiling.

6 Add other ingredients to the pot as needed while eating, dipping in lemon-soy sauce with condiments to taste.

◆ INGREDIENTS (4 servings)

2 1/4 lb chicken thighs
　with bones
6 (10 1/2 oz) leaves
　Chinese cabbage
1 bunch (7 oz) spinach
8 fresh *shiitake* mushrooms
2 Japanese leeks
4 rice cakes, 1-inch square
Konbu Kelp *Dashi*
　⌈ 8 1/3 U.S. cups water
　⌊ 1 3/4 oz *konbu* kelp
Lemon-Soy Sauce (or *Ponzu*)
　⌈ 5 oz lemon juice
　| 5 oz soy sauce
　| 3 Tbsp boild *saké*
　⌊ 1 Tbsp boild *mirin*
Condiments
　⌈ rinsed scallions (→p. 33)
　| grated *daikon* radish
　⌊ chili pepper flakes

湯豆腐

1人分 160 kcal

◆材　料 (4人分)

豆腐　2丁 (600 g)
昆布だし
├ 水　1000 cc
└ 昆布　30 g
つけじょうゆ
├ だし　250 cc
├ しょうゆ　100 cc
└ みりん　大さじ2
薬味
├ さらしねぎ (→32頁)
├ おろししょうが
├ 糸花がつお
├ 白ごま
└ もみのり　など適当に

◆作り方

1 昆布は布巾でさっとふいて、汚れを落とす。食卓に出せる鍋に分量の水と昆布を入れ、3時間おく。

2 豆腐は3cm角に切る。

3 つけじょうゆの材料を一煮立ちさせ、器に入れる。

4 薬味を用意する。

5 1の鍋を火にかけ、弱火で豆腐をコトコト煮る。

6 つけじょうゆに好みの薬味を入れて食べる。

Simmered Tofu
Yu-dōfu

160 kcal per serving

◆ DIRECTIONS

1 Wipe *konbu* kelp lightly with cheesecloth to clean. Place water and *konbu* kelp in a large pot that is presentable for the table; let stand for 3 hours.

2 Cut tofu into 1-inch cubes.

3 Place dipping sauce ingredients in a saucepan, bring to a boil, and transfer to a serving bowl.

4 Prepare condiments.

5 Place pot over low heat and simmer tofu.

6 Add condiments to dipping sauce when eating.

◆ INGREDIENTS (4 servings)

2 cakes (21 oz) tofu

Konbu Kelp *Dashi*
- 4 U.S. cups water
- 1 oz *konbu* kelp

Dipping Sauce
- 1 U.S. cup *dashi*
- 3¹/₃ oz soy sauce
- 2 Tbsp *mirin*

Condiments
- rinsed scallions (→p. 33)
- grated fresh ginger
- bonito threads
- white sesame seeds
- crumbled toasted *nori* seaweed

お好み焼き

1人分 500 kcal

◆材 料 (4人分)

豚ばら肉 (薄切り) 100 g
いか (上身) 100 g
キャベツ 200 g
青ねぎ 4本
紅しょうが酢漬け (刻む)
　大さじ2
生地
　小麦粉　150 g
　水　150 cc
　山の芋 (おろす)　80 g
　卵　4個
　塩　小さじ½
サラダ油　適量
お好み焼きソース (市販品)
　適量
粉がつお　適量
青のり　適量
マヨネーズ　適量

◆作り方

1　豚肉は7〜8cm幅に切り、いかは
細切りにする。キャベツ、青ねぎは
粗いみじん切りにする。

2　生地を作る。小麦粉、水、山の芋、
塩を泡立て器で混ぜ、溶き卵を加え、
さっと合わせる。

3　いか、キャベツ、青ねぎを加えて、
よく混ぜ合わせる。

4　1人分ずつ焼く。鉄板に油を熱し、
豚肉をさっと焼き、生地をのせ、
紅しょうがを散らす。上面が半乾きになり
プツプツと穴があき、下側をのぞいて、
こんがりと焼き色がついてきたらひっくり
返し、もう片面も焼く。

5　お好み焼きソースを塗り、粉がつおと
青のりをふりかける。好みでマヨネーズを
つける。

メモ
• 具にきまりはない。生地に好みの肉、魚介、
野菜など手近な材料を合わせて焼けば
お好み焼き。

"As-You-Like-It" Pancake

Okonomi-yaki

500 kcal per serving

◆ DIRECTIONS

1 Cut pork into 3-inch pieces, slice squid into thin strips, mince cabbage and scallions coarsely.

2 Using a whisk, make batter, combining flour, water, grated mountain yam, and salt. Add beaten eggs, stir lightly.

3 Add squid, cabbage, scallions, and mix well.

4 Divide all ingredients into 4 portions. Oil griddle. Sauté pork briefly and pour batter over, then sprinkle with pickled ginger. When the surface bubbles and the bottom is golden brown, turn over and brown the other side.

5 Brush with *okonomi-yaki* sauce, sprinkle with bonito powder and *ao-nori* flakes. Serve with mayonnaise to taste.

NOTE
• Ingredients may vary. Cook any meat, seafood, vegetables with the batter "as you like it."

◆ INGREDIENTS (4 servings)

3 1/2 oz pork belly,
   thinly sliced
3 1/2 oz squid (body only)
7 oz cabbage
4 scallions
2 Tbsp red pickled ginger,
   finely chopped
Batter
   5 1/4 oz flour
   5 oz water
   2 4/5 oz grated mountain
      yam
   4 eggs
   1/2 tsp salt
vegetable oil
Topping
   okonomi-yaki sauce
   dried bonito powder
   ao-nori (green-seaweed)
      flakes
   mayonnaise

焼きなす

1人分 150 kcal

◆材　料(4人分)

なす (150 gのもの)　4個
オクラ　8本
塩　適量
かけつゆ
┌ しょうゆ　50 cc
│ だし　大さじ1
└ しょうがの絞り汁　小さじ1
糸花がつお　適量

◆作り方

1　なすは焼き網にのせ、強火で
皮一面をころがすようにして焼く。
押してみて充分に柔らかくなったら、
水に入れ、手早く皮をむく。へたを
切り落とし、縦に5つ〜6つに手でさき、
5cm長さに切る。→❶❷

2　オクラはへたを切り落とし、塩もみして、
たっぷりの熱湯で塩ゆでにする。
ざるに上げてさまし、縦半分に切って種を
除き、刻む。

3　かけつゆの材料を合わせる。

4　器になすとオクラを盛り、かけつゆを
かけ、糸花がつおをのせる。

❶

❷

Grilled Eggplant
Yaki-Nasu

150 kcal per serving

◆ DIRECTIONS

1   Grill eggplants on a cooking grill over high heat, rolling them. Test by pressing with finger, and when tender, plunge into cold water and peel quickly. Remove stems, tear into 5–6 long pieces by hand, and cut into 2-inch lengths. →❶❷

2   Remove stems from okra, rub with salt, and parboil in ample hot water. Drain in a sieve, and let cool. Cut in half lengthwise, remove seeds, and chop finely.

3   Combine sauce ingredients.

4   Place eggplant and okra in serving dishes, pour sauce over, and garnish with bonito threads.

◆ INGREDIENTS (4 servings)

4 eggplants, 5¼ oz each
8 pods okra
salt
Sauce
 ⌈ 1⅔ oz soy sauce
 ⎱ 1 Tbsp *dashi*
 ⌊ 1 tsp fresh ginger juice
dried bonito threads

だし巻き卵

1人分 180 kcal

◆材　料(4人分)

卵　8個
だし　100 cc
みりん　大さじ1
しょうゆ　大さじ1
塩　小さじ½
サラダ油　適量
大根おろし　適量
しょうゆ　適量

◆作り方

1　卵はよく溶きほぐす。

2　だしに調味料をよく溶かし、卵に混ぜる。

3　卵焼き鍋の四隅まで油を塗り、卵液を落とすとジュッと音がするくらい温める。

4　卵液を少量流し込んで全体に広げる。→❶

5　半熟程度になったら手前に巻き上げる。鍋のあいたところに油をひく。→❷

6　卵を向こう側にすべらせ、あいたところに油をひき、再び卵液を流し込む。これをくり返し、少しずつ巻いて厚くしていく。→❸❹

7　熱いうちに巻き簀で巻き、切り分ける。→❺

8　器に盛り、大根おろしにしょうゆを少し落として添える。

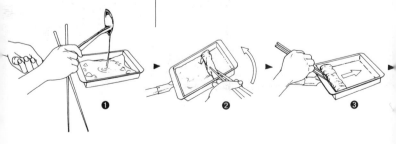

❶　　　　❷　　　　❸

Rolled Omelette

Dashi-maki Tamago

180 kcal per serving

◆ DIRECTIONS

1 Beat eggs well in a bowl.

2 Add *mirin*, soy sauce, and salt to *dashi*, mix well, then blend into beaten eggs.

3 Coat a square omelette pan with oil, and heat until a drop of egg mixture sizzles.

4 Pour in a small portion of egg mixture and spread evenly. →❶

5 When the mixture is half done, roll toward front of the pan and grease empty space in the pan. →❷

6 Slide roll to the other end, grease empty space again, and add more of the egg mixture. Repeat this, making the roll bigger. →❸❹

7 When egg roll is done, shape evenly by using a bamboo rolling mat, and cut into pieces. →❺

8 Serve omelette pieces with grated *daikon*, and add a dash of soy sauce.

◆ INGREDIENTS (4 servings)

8 eggs
3 1/3 oz *dashi*
1 Tbsp *mirin*
1 Tbsp soy sauce
1/2 tsp salt
vegetable oil
Garnish
{ grated *daikon* radish
{ dash soy sauce

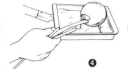

❹

❺

焼きはまぐり

1人分 20 kcal

◆材　料(4人分)

はまぐり (60 gのもの)　12個
塩　適量

◆作り方

1　はまぐりは塩水(水200ccに塩小さじ1の割合)につけて、砂を吐かせる。

2　貝殻をこすりつけて、よく洗う。

3　殻と殻のつなぎ目の靱帯を切り、貝殻に塩をまぶす。→❶

4　焼き網にのせ、強火で焼く。→❷

5　口が開いたら、火からおろし、器に盛る*。

＊盛りつけるとき、塩を敷くと安定する。

Salt-Grilled Clams

Yaki-Hamaguri

20 kcal per serving

◆ DIRECTIONS

1   Soak clams in salted water (1 tsp salt to 6⅔ oz water) to let them expel sand.

2   Wash well, rubbing shells against each other.

3   Cut off black hinge ligaments, and sprinkle salt on the outside of shells. →❶

4   Grill clams on a cooking grill over high heat. →❷

5   When clams are open, remove from heat, and arrange on serving plates.*

∗ Place the clams on a bed of salt to secure.

◆ INGREDIENTS (4 servings)

12 live hard-shell clams,
   2 oz each
salt

ぶりの照り焼き

1人分 480 kcal

◆材 料(4人分)

ぶり(150 gの切り身)
　4切れ
塩　適量
小麦粉　適量
サラダ油　適量
照り焼きのたれ
　砂糖　大さじ2
　みりん　大さじ4
　酒　大さじ4
　しょうゆ　100 cc
菊花かぶ甘酢漬け
　(→114頁)　4個

◆作り方

1　ぶりは薄く塩をふり、30分ほどおく。

2　洗って水けをふき取り、小麦粉を薄くまぶす。

3　フライパンに油少量を熱し、ぶりの両面をしっかり焼く。

4　ぶりを取り出し、たれの材料を入れて少し煮つめる。

5　ぶりをもどして、たれをすくいかけ、照りよく仕上げる。→❶

6　器に盛り、菊花かぶを添える。

❶

Yellowtail Teriyaki
Buri no Teriyaki

480 kcal per serving

◆ DIRECTIONS

1 Sprinkle yellowtail fillets with salt lightly, and let stand for 30 minutes.

2 Rinse the fillets, pat dry, and coat with flour.

3 Heat oil in a frying pan, and fry the fillets until both sides are golden brown.

4 Remove the fillets, add all the teriyaki sauce ingredients, and simmer it down slightly.

5 Return the fillets to the pan and spoon over teriyaki sauce until the fish glazed.→❶

6 Place the fillets on serving plates, garnish with chrysanthemum turnips.

◆ INGREDIENTS (4 servings)

4 yellowtail fillets,
  5 1/4 oz each
salt
flour
vegetable oil
Teriyaki Sauce
  ⎰ 2 Tbsp sugar
  ⎰ 4 Tbsp *mirin*
  ⎰ 4 Tbsp *saké*
  ⎱ 3 1/3 oz soy sauce
4 chrysanthemum turnips
  (→p. 115)

焼きとり

1人分 290 kcal

◆材　料(4人分)

鶏もも肉 (骨なし)　400 g
長ねぎ　1本
ピーマン　2個
サラダ油　適量
焼きとりのたれ
　　砂糖　大さじ2
　　みりん　大さじ4
　　酒　大さじ4
　　しょうゆ　100 cc
七味唐がらし、または
　　粉ざんしょう　少々

◆作り方

1　鶏肉は2cm角に切る。長ねぎ、ピーマンも同じ大きさに切る。

2　竹串に鶏肉と長ねぎ、ピーマンを交互に刺す。

3　フライパンに油を熱し、鶏肉の全体に焼き色をつけ、弱火にして中まで火を通す。

4　串を取り出し、たれの材料を入れて煮つめる。

5　串をもどし、たれをからめる。

6　器に盛り、好みで七味唐がらし、粉ざんしょうをふる。

Yakitori

290 kcal per serving

◆ DIRECTIONS

1 Cut chicken into ¾-inch squares. Cut leek and bell peppers roughly the same size as chicken.

2 Skewer chicken, leek, and bell pepper on bamboo skewers.

3 Heat oil in a frying pan, brown the skewered food, lower the heat, and cook down.

4 Remove the skewered food, add sauce, and simmer it down.

5 Return the skewers to the pan and coat with the sauce.

6 Arrange the food on plates, sprinkle with seven-spice pepper or ground *sansho* pepper.

◆ INGREDIENTS (4 servings)

14 oz boned chicken thigh
1 Japanese leek
2 green bell peppers
vegetable oil
Yakitori Sauce
  2 Tbsp sugar
  4 Tbsp *mirin*
  4 Tbsp *saké*
  3⅓ oz soy sauce
seven-spice pepper or
  ground *sansho* pepper

牛肉の照り焼き

1人分 560 kcal

◆材　料 (4人分)

牛ロース肉 (150 gのもの)
　4枚

こしょう　少々

サラダ油　適量

照り焼きのたれ

　砂糖　大さじ2
　みりん　大さじ4
　酒　大さじ4
　しょうゆ　100 cc

つけ合わせ

　貝割れ菜 (貝割れ大根)
　　50 g
　プチトマト　8個

練りがらし　適量

◆作り方

1　牛肉に軽くこしょうをふる。

2　フライパンに油少量を熱し、牛肉の
両面に焼き色をつける。好みの
焼きかげんになったら、牛肉を一度
取り出す。

3　たれの材料をフライパンに入れ、
煮つめる。

4　牛肉をもどし、たれをからめながら、
照りよく仕上げる。

5　一口大に切って器に盛り、生野菜を
つけ合わせ、からしを添える。

Steak Teriyaki
Gyūniku no Teriyaki

560 kcal per serving

◆ DIRECTIONS

1 Sprinkle beef with pepper lightly.

2 Heat oil in a frying pan, and brown both sides of the beef. When the beef is done to your preference, remove from pan.

3 Add all teriyaki sauce ingredients, and simmer it down.

4 Return the beef to the pan, and continue turning until glazed.

5 Cut the meat into bite-sized pieces, mound on serving plates, and garnish with vegetables. Serve with mustard.

◆ INGREDIENTS (4 servings)

4 beef sirloin steaks,
  5 1/4 oz each
pinch pepper
vegetable oil
Teriyaki Sauce
  2 Tbsp sugar
  4 Tbsp *mirin*
  4 Tbsp *saké*
  3 1/3 oz soy sauce
Garnish
  1 3/4 oz *daikon* radish
    sprouts
  8 cherry tomatoes
mustard

豚肉のしょうが焼き

1人分 280 kcal

◆材 料(4人分)

豚ロース肉 (薄切り)　400 g

グリーンアスパラガス　8本

塩　少々

しょうがのたれ

- 砂糖　大さじ1
- みりん　大さじ2
- 酒　大さじ2
- しょうゆ　大さじ4
- しょうが (みじん切り)
  大さじ1

サラダ油　適量

こしょう　適量

◆作り方

1　豚肉は半分に切る。

2　グリーンアスパラガスは根元を
たわめてみて、ポキッと折れるところで
折り、下の方のかたい皮をむいて、
5cm長さに切り、塩ゆでにする。

3　たれの材料を混ぜ合わせておく。

4　フライパンに油少量を熱し、豚肉を
広げて入れ、両面を焼く。アスパラガスを
加えていため、軽くこしょうをふる。

5　たれを加え、からめて仕上げる。

6　器に豚肉を盛り、アスパラガスを
添える。

Ginger Pork Sauté

Butaniku no Shōga-yaki

280 kcal per serving

◆ DIRECTIONS

1 Cut the pork slices in half.

2 Break off the woody ends and peel the lower part of asparagus, cut into 2-inch lengths, and boil in lightly salted water.

3 Combine ginger sauce ingredients.

4 Heat oil in a frying pan, sauté pork (spreading evenly), till brown on both sides. Add asparagus, and sauté briefly. Sprinkle with pepper.

5 Add sauce, and stir to coat pork and asparagus.

6 Arrange pork and asparagus on serving plates.

◆ INGREDIENTS (4 servings)

14 oz pork loin,
   thinly sliced
8 green asparagus stalks
pinch salt
Ginger Sauce
   1 Tbsp sugar
   2 Tbsp *mirin*
   2 Tbsp *saké*
   4 Tbsp soy sauce
   1 Tbsp finely minced
      fresh ginger
vegetable oil
pepper

さけのポテトサラダ包み焼き

1人分 320 kcal

◆**材 料**(4人分)

さけ (100 gの切り身)
　4切れ
塩、こしょう　各適量
ポテトサラダ
　じゃが芋
　　2～3個 (300 g)
　にんじん　½本 (100 g)
　きゅうり　1本 (120 g)
　玉ねぎ　½個 (70 g)
　マヨネーズ　50 g
　塩、こしょう　各適量
バター　適量
レモンのくし形切り　4個

◆**作り方**

1　さけは厚みに包丁を入れて2枚に開き、両面に軽く塩、こしょうをふり、20分おく。

2　じゃが芋は四つ割りに、にんじんは縦半分に切り、たっぷりの水に入れてゆで、柔らかくなったら湯を捨てる。再び火にかけ、鍋をゆすりながら水分をとばし、粉ふきにする。じゃが芋は薄切りに、にんじんはいちょう切りにする。

3　きゅうり、玉ねぎは薄切りにして、塩をふり、軽くもんで余分な水けを絞る。

4　じゃが芋、にんじん、きゅうり、玉ねぎを合わせ、マヨネーズ、塩、こしょうで味を調える。

5　アルミ箔の中央にバターを塗り、ポテトサラダ¼量をのせ、さけで包んで形を整え、アルミ箔で包む。→❶

6　170～180℃のオーブンで20分焼く。

7　器に盛り、レモンを添える。

❶

Stuffed Salmon

Sake no Poteto Sarada Tsutsumi-yaki

320 kcal per serving

◆ DIRECTIONS

1   Cut almost completely through the fillet from the side. Spread open, sprinkle with salt and pepper on both sides, and let stand 20 minutes.

2   Cut potatoes into 4 pieces, cut carrot in half lengthwise. Place in ample boiling water until tender, and drain. Return to heat, shaking to evaporate excess water and cooking until the surface of the potatoes has a powdery texture. Cut potatoes into thin slices and carrot into quarter-rounds.

3   Cut cucumber and onion into thin slices, sprinkle with salt, and squeeze lightly to remove excess moisture.

4   Combine potatoes, carrot, cucumber, and onion. Add mayonnaise, salt and pepper to season.

5   Grease 4 ½-inch square sheets of aluminum foil with butter. Mound potato salad in the center of each sheet, wrap salmon around the mounds, and close up the foil to make neat packages. → ❶

6   Bake the packages in oven at 340–360°F for 20 minutes.

7   Transfer the packages to serving plates, and garnish with lemon wedges.

◆ INGREDIENTS (4 servings)

4 salmon fillets,
   3 1/2 oz each
salt and pepper
Potato Salad
⎡ 2–3 (10 1/2 oz) potatoes
  1/2 (3 1/2 oz) carrot
  1 (4 1/5 oz) cucumber
  1/2 (2 1/2 oz) onion
  1 3/4 oz mayonnaise
⎣ salt and pepper
butter
4 wedges lemon

豆腐田楽

1人分 220 kcal

◆材　料(4人分)

木綿豆腐　2丁 (600 g)
田楽みそ
[赤みそ　100 g
  酒　100 cc
  砂糖　大さじ3
  卵黄　1個]
サラダ油　適量
木の芽 (葉のみ)　適量

◆作り方

1　豆腐は布巾にはさみ、軽い重石をし、斜めにして30分水きりをする。→❶

2　小鍋に田楽みその材料を混ぜ合わせ、弱火でポッテリと練り上げる。

3　1の豆腐を3cm幅で5cm長さ、2cm厚さに切る。あれば田楽串に刺す。

4　フライパンに油少量を熱し、中火で豆腐の両面に焼き色をつける。

5　器に盛り、温かい田楽みそを塗って、木の芽を散らす。

メモ
• 田楽とは串に刺して焼き、みそを塗った料理のこと。
• なす、こんにゃく、里芋の田楽もおいしい。好みでゆずみそ(170頁参照)でも。

Tofu *Dengaku*

220 kcal per serving

◆ DIRECTIONS

1   Place each cake of tofu between two cloth kitchen towels, weight lightly, and let stand on a slightly tilted surface for 30 minutes to drain. →❶

2   Combine all *dengaku* miso topping ingredients in a small pot, and mix well. Stir over low heat until thick.

3   Cut pressed tofu into 1 1/8 × 2 × 3/4-inch pieces. If *dengaku* skewers are available, skewer tofu pieces.

4   Heat oil in a frying pan over medium heat, and brown both sides of the tofu pieces.

5   Arrange on serving plates, spread with hot *dengaku* topping, and sprinkle with *kinome* leaves.

NOTE
• *Dengaku* means skewered and grilled food with miso topping. Eggplants, *konnyaku* (devil's tongue jelly), and taros are also highly recommended for *dengaku*. *Yuzu*-miso sauce (p. 171) can also be used.

◆ INGREDIENTS (4 servings)

2 cakes (21 oz) "cotton" tofu

Dengaku Miso Topping
  3 1/2 oz red miso
  3 1/3 oz saké
  3 Tbsp sugar
  I egg yolk
vegetable oil
kinome sprigs, stemmed

❶

里芋の煮っころがし

1人分 130 kcal

◆材　料 (4人分)

里芋　12個 (600 g)
米のとぎ汁 (またはガーゼに
　　米大さじ1～2を包んで)
煮汁
[だし　400 cc
　砂糖　大さじ3
　みりん　大さじ2
　しょうゆ　大さじ3]

◆作り方

1　里芋はよく洗って、両端を切り落として、
皮をむく。

2　米のとぎ汁で、下ゆでする。

3　鍋に里芋、だし、砂糖、みりんを
入れて、落としぶた*をして火にかける。
約10分煮て、しょうゆを加えてゆっくり
煮る。

4　鍋をゆすって煮汁をからめ、ころがして
つやよく仕上げる。

＊落としぶた：煮物を作るとき、鍋の中の
材料に直接のせるふたのことで、鍋の直径より
小さくする。ふたにあたって、煮汁がよく行き
渡り、味が充分しみ込み、また早く煮上げるこ
とができる。ふつう木製であるが、ステンレス製、
ガラス製、アルミ箔、和紙などを使ってもよい。

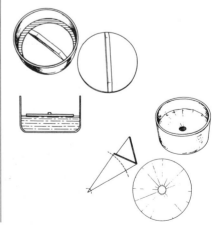

Taro Tumbles

Satoimo no Ni-kkorogashi

130 kcal per serving

◆ DIRECTIONS

1 Wash taros thoroughly, cut both ends off, and peel.

2 Parboil taros in water used to rinse rice.

3 Place the taros, *dashi*, sugar, and *mirin* in a soup pot, cover with a drop-lid*, and heat over medium heat. Cook for 10 minutes, add soy sauce, and simmer it down.

4 Shake the pot to tumble the taros, coating them with glaze.

∗ Drop-lids: A drop-lid, which is smaller than the diameter of the pan, is placed directly on the ingredients or liquid inside the pan, mainly for simmering. Bubbling liquid is forced back down by hitting the lid, and circulates evenly. Flavor distributes well, and the contents cook quickly. Wooden lids are usually used, however, stainless steel or glass lids, aluminum foil, or *washi* (Japanese paper) are also fine.

◆ INGREDIENTS (4 servings)

12 (21 oz) taros
water used to rinse rice,
   or water and 1–2 Tbsp
   rice wrapped in
   cheesecloth
Stock
  ⌈ 1²/3 U.S. cup *dashi*
  │ 3 Tbsp sugar
  │ 2 Tbsp *mirin*
  ⌊ 3 Tbsp soy sauce

肉じゃが

`1人分 300 kcal`

◆材 料 (4人分)

牛ばら肉 (薄切り)　150 g
じゃが芋　4個 (600 g)
糸こんにゃく　½袋 (100 g)
玉ねぎ　1個 (150 g)
さやいんげん　10本
塩　少々
サラダ油　適量
煮汁
- だし　800 cc
- 酒　100 cc
- 砂糖　大さじ4
- みりん　大さじ2
- しょうゆ　大さじ5

◆作り方

1　牛肉は3〜4cm長さに切る。

2　じゃが芋は4つ〜6つに切り、水にさらす。

3　糸こんにゃくは5〜6cm長さに切る。玉ねぎは縦半分に切り、横にして1cm幅に切る。

4　さやいんげんは塩ゆでし、3cm長さに切る。

5　鍋に油少量を熱し、牛肉を軽くいため、じゃが芋、糸こんにゃく、玉ねぎを加えてよくいためる。

6　だしを加えて、じゃが芋が柔らかくなったら調味料を加え、中火で15分煮る。

7　器に盛り、さやいんげんを散らす。

Braised Meat and Potatoes

Niku-jaga

300 kcal per serving

◆ DIRECTIONS

1 Cut beef into 1½-inch lengths.

2 Cut potatoes into 4–6 pieces each, and soak in cold water.

3 Cut *ito-konnyaku* into 2-inch lengths. Cut onion in half top to bottom, slice into ⅜-inch half rings.

4 Parboil green beans, and cut into 1-inch lengths.

5 Heat oil in a skillet, stir-fry beef lightly. Add potatoes, *ito-konnyaku*, and onion, and continue stir-frying.

6 Add *dashi*, cook until potatoes are tender, and add seasonings. Cook over medium heat for 15 minutes.

7 Serve in a bowl with green beans sprinkled on top.

◆ INGREDIENTS (4 servings)

5¼ oz beef sirloin, thinly sliced

4 (21 oz) potatoes

½ pack (3½ oz) *ito-konnyaku* (devil's tongue jelly filaments)

1 (5¼ oz) onion

10 green beans

pinch salt

vegetable oil

Stock
- 3⅓ U.S. cups *dashi*
- 3⅓ oz *saké*
- 4 Tbsp sugar
- 2 Tbsp *mirin*
- 5 Tbsp soy sauce

きんぴらごぼう

1人分 90 kcal

◆**材 料**(4人分)

ごぼう　2本 (150 g)
ごま油　大さじ2
煮汁
 ┌ 砂糖　小さじ1
 │ 酒　大さじ2
 └ しょうゆ　50 cc
いりごま　適量
一味唐がらし　適量

◆**作り方**

1　ごぼうはよく洗い、細い方から
削るように粗い笹がきにする*。水で
さっと洗い、水けをよくきる。

2　鍋にごま油を熱し、ごぼうを強火で
いためる。

3　煮汁を加え、汁けがほとんどなくなる
までいりつける。

4　器に盛り、好みでいりごま、
一味唐がらしをふる。

＊笹がきごぼう: 鉛筆
を削る要領で、包丁を
ねかせ、ごぼうを
回しながら切る。

メモ
• きんぴらとは、油でいため、砂糖、しょうゆ
などでいり煮する料理。
• ごぼうの代わりに、にんじん、れんこん、
セロリのきんぴらもおいしい。

Sautéed Burdock, *Kimpira*-style

Kinpira Gobō

| 90 kcal per serving |

◆ DIRECTIONS

1 Wash burdock roots well, and shave coarsely from the skinnier ends.* Rinse briefly with water, and drain.

2 Heat sesame oil in a frying pan, and stir-fry burdock over high heat.

3 Add all sauce ingredients, and cook down until almost all the liquid is evaporated.

4 Serve in small dishes with toasted sesame seeds and chili pepper flakes sprinkled on top to taste.

*To shave burdock roots: Cut them as if sharpening a pencil. An easy method is to lay them side by side on a cutting board and alternately roll them slightly and make oblique cuts.

NOTES
• *Kimpira* is a cooking style involving stir-frying and simmering with sugar and soy sauce.
• Carrots, lotus roots, and celery are also delicious for *kimpira*.

◆ INGREDIENTS (4 servings)

2 (5 1/4 oz) burdock roots
2 Tbsp sesame oil
Sauce
⎰ I tsp sugar
⎱ 2 Tbsp *saké*
⎰ 1 2/3 oz soy sauce
toasted sesame seeds
chili pepper flakes

かぼちゃと厚揚げの煮物

1人分 210 kcal

◆材 料(4人分)

かぼちゃ ½個 (500 g)
厚揚げ 2枚 (200 g)
煮汁
  だし 800 cc
  みりん 100 cc
  砂糖 大さじ2
  酒 大さじ4
  薄口しょうゆ 大さじ6
しょうが (せん切り) 20 g

◆作り方

1 かぼちゃは3〜4cm角に切り、皮を
ところどころむく。→❶

2 厚揚げは熱湯に通して油抜きし、
3cm角に切る。

3 鍋にかぼちゃの皮を下にして並べ、
厚揚げ、煮汁の材料を入れ、落としぶた
をして強火にかける。沸騰したら弱火に
し、柔らかくなるまで約30分煮る。→❷

4 器に盛り、しょうがのせん切りを
のせる。

❶

❷

Simmered Acorn Squash with Deep-Fried Tofu

Kabocha to Atsuage no Nimono

210 kcal per serving

◆ DIRECTIONS

1 Cut squash into 1½-inch blocks, and peel, leaving some skin on.→❶

2 Dip deep-fried tofu in hot water to remove excess oil, and cut into 1-inch cubes.

3 Place squash in a skillet with the skin side down, add tofu and all the cooking sauce ingredients, cover with a drop-lid, and heat on high. Lower the heat when mixture boils, and simmer for 30 minutes until tender.→❷

4 Serve in small bowls and top with slivered ginger.

◆ INGREDIENTS (4 servings)

½ (18 oz) acorn squash
2 cakes (7 oz) "thick" deep-fried tofu (*atsuage*)
Sauce
  3⅓ U.S. cups *dashi*
  3⅓ oz *mirin*
  2 Tbsp sugar
  4 Tbsp *saké*
  6 Tbsp light soy sauce
⅔ oz fresh ginger, finely slivered

白菜と薄揚げの旨煮

1人分 130 kcal

◆材 料(4人分)

白菜 ¼株(500 g)
薄揚げ 2枚(60 g)
しょうが 20 g
煮汁
  だし 600 cc
  砂糖 大さじ3
  みりん 大さじ2
  薄口しょうゆ 大さじ4
  塩 小さじ¼

◆作り方

1 白菜の葉はざく切り、芯は2cm幅の短冊切りにする。

2 薄揚げは熱湯に通して油抜きをし、白菜と同じ大きさの短冊切りにする。

3 しょうがはせん切りにする。

4 鍋に煮汁の材料を入れて煮立て、白菜、薄揚げ、しょうがを加えて、中火で柔らかくなるまで約10分煮る。

Simmered Chinese Cabbage with Deep-Fried Tofu

Hakusai to Usuage no Uma-ni

130 kcal per serving

◆ DIRECTIONS

1 Cut cabbage leaves roughly into pieces, and stalks into ¾-inch strips.

2 Dip deep-fried tofu in hot water to remove excess oil, and cut into ¾-inch strips.

3 Cut ginger into fine slivers.

4 Combine all sauce ingredients in a skillet, bring to a boil, add cabbage, tofu, and ginger. Cook over medium heat for 10 minutes until tender.

◆ INGREDIENTS (4 servings)

¼ (18 oz) Chinese cabbage
2 sheets (2 oz) "thin" deep-fried tofu (*usuage*)
⅔ oz fresh ginger
Sauce
  2½ U.S. cups *dashi*
  3 Tbsp sugar
  2 Tbsp *mirin*
  4 Tbsp light soy sauce
  ¼ tsp salt

ひじきのいため煮

1人分 130 kcal

◆材 料(4人分)

ひじき(乾燥) 30 g
鶏もも肉 100 g
サラダ油 大さじ1
煮汁
  だし 400 cc
  酒 大さじ2
  砂糖 大さじ2
  みりん 大さじ3
  しょうゆ 大さじ5

◆作り方

1 ひじきはたっぷりの水でよく洗い、
ごみや砂を沈ませ、ざるにすくい上げる。
ぬるま湯に30分つけてもどす。
もう一度水でよく洗い、ざるに上げて
水けをきる。→❶

2 鶏肉は1cm角のさいの目に切る。

3 鍋にサラダ油を熱し、鶏肉、ひじきの
順でいためる。

4 煮汁を加え、煮汁がほぼなくなるまで
(約15～20分)弱火で煮つめる。

❶

Braised *Hijiki* Seaweed

Hijiki no Itame-ni

130 kcal per serving

◆ DIRECTIONS

1 Wash *hijiki* seaweed well in ample water, letting sand and unwanted particles sink to the bottom of the bowl, and scoop *hijiki* up in a strainer. Soak *hijiki* in lukewarm water for 30 minutes. Rinse again in water, and drain.→❶

2 Cut chicken into ⅜-inch cubes.

3 Heat oil in a skillet, stir-fry chicken, then add *hijiki*.

4 Add all sauce ingredients, and cook over low heat for 15–20 minutes, until the sauce is almost gone.

◆ INGREDIENTS (4 servings)

1 oz dried *hijiki* seaweed
3½ oz chicken thighs
1 Tbsp vegetable oil
Sauce
  1⅔ U.S. cups *dashi*
  2 Tbsp *saké*
  2 Tbsp sugar
  3 Tbsp *mirin*
  5 Tbsp soy sauce

高野豆腐の含め煮

^{こうや}

```
1人分 160 kcal
```

◆材 料(4人分)

高野豆腐 (=凍り豆腐)　4枚

煮汁

- だし　500 cc
- 砂糖　大さじ3
- みりん　大さじ2
- 薄口しょうゆ　大さじ3
- 塩　小さじ½

◆作り方

1　高野豆腐はバットなどに並べ、約80℃の湯をたっぷり注ぐ。途中で表裏を返し、中心を指ではさんで芯がなくなったら、再びたっぷりの水につけ、水の中で高野豆腐を手のひらにはさみ、水けを押し出す。白く濁った水が出なくなるまで何回もくり返す。→❶❷

2　鍋にだしと水けを充分に絞った高野豆腐を入れ、沸騰したら火を弱め、砂糖とみりんを加えて約10分煮る。

3　薄口しょうゆと塩を加えて約20分煮、そのままさまして味を含ませる。

4　食べやすい大きさに切り、器に盛る。

❶

❷

Simmered Freeze-Dried Tofu

Kōya-dōfu no Fukume-ni

160 kcal per serving

◆ DIRECTIONS

1   Place *koya-dofu* in a square cake pan with ample hot water (180°F). Turn tofu over, and when the center is soft, soak it in cold water. In the soaking bowl, press tofu between your hands to squeeze out water. Repeat until whitish liquid stops coming out of *koya-dofu*. →❶❷

2   Place dashi and well-wrung *koya-dofu* in a skillet, bring to a boil, and then lower heat. Add sugar and mirin, and cook for 10 minutes.

3   Add light soy sauce and salt, cook for 20 minutes, and remove from heat. Let stand to cool and distribute flavor.

4   Cut *koya-dofu* into bite-sized pieces, and serve.

◆ INGREDIENTS (4 servings)

4 cakes *koya-dofu*
  (freeze-dried tofu)
Sauce
  2 1/8 U.S. cups *dashi*
  3 Tbsp sugar
  2 Tbsp *mirin*
  3 Tbsp light soy sauce
  1/2 tsp salt

ふろふき大根

1人分 130 kcal

◆材 料 (4人分)

大根 (2cm厚さの輪切り)
　8切れ
米のとぎ汁 (または米大さじ1
　〜2をガーゼに包んでも可)
昆布　8cm
ゆずみそ
　┌白みそ　100g
　│砂糖　大さじ2
　│酒　大さじ2
　│だし　大さじ4
　│卵黄　1個
　└ゆず　½個

◆作り方

1　大根は皮を厚くむき、底に十文字の
切り込みを入れる。→❶

2　米のとぎ汁に入れて火にかけ、
ややかために下ゆでし、水洗いする。

3　鍋に昆布を敷いて大根を並べ、
ひたひたの水で柔らかくなるまでゆでる。

4　ゆずは白い部分が入らないように
表皮だけをおろす。→❷

5　小鍋にゆず以外のゆずみその材料を
入れ、弱火でポッテリと練り上げる。火を
とめて、ゆずを混ぜ合わせる。

6　器に熱々の大根を盛り、熱いゆずみそ
をかける。

Boiled Radish with Miso Sauce

Furofuki Daikon

130 kcal per serving

◆ DIRECTIONS

1 Peel *daikon*, and score a cross on one side. →**❶**

2 Parboil *daikon* in water used to rinse rice, then rinse with cold water.

3 Place *konbu* kelp in a pot, set *daikon*, on top of *konbu*, add water just to cover *daikon*, and cook until tender.

4 Grate *yuzu* citron rind. →**❷**

5 Combine all miso sauce ingredients except *yuzu*, and place over low heat, stirring until thick. Remove from heat, and add grated *yuzu* rind.

6 Arrange hot radish in serving bowls, pour on hot *yuzu*-miso sauce.

◆ INGREDIENTS (4 servings)

8 round slices (³/₄-inch thick) of *daikon* radish
water used to rinse rice, or water and 1–2 Tbsp rice wrapped in cheesecloth
3-inch square *konbu* kelp
Yuzu-Miso Sauce
  3¹/₂ oz white miso
  2 Tbsp sugar
  2 Tbsp *saké*
  4 Tbsp *dashi*
  1 egg yolk
  ¹/₂ *yuzu* citron

❶

❷

筑前煮

1人分 230 kcal

◆材 料(4人分)

鶏もも肉 (骨なし)　400 g
にんじん　1本 (150 g)
ごぼう　1本 (100 g)
れんこん　5 cm (100 g)
生しいたけ　4枚
ピーマン　2個
こんにゃく　½枚 (125 g)
サラダ油　適量
煮汁
　だし　600 cc
　砂糖　大さじ2
　みりん　大さじ3
　しょうゆ　大さじ5

◆作り方

1　鶏肉は一口大に切る。

2　にんじん、ごぼう、れんこんは
乱切りにし、しいたけは軸を取り、
四つ割りにする。

3　ピーマンは縦に四つ割りにし、へたと
種を取り、横に1cm幅に切る。

4　こんにゃくは一口大に手でちぎり、
さっとゆでる。

5　鍋にサラダ油を熱し、鶏肉、にんじん、
ごぼう、れんこん、こんにゃく、しいたけの
順に加えてよくいためる。

6　だし、砂糖、みりんを加え、
落としぶたをして始め強火、煮立ったら
弱火にする。アクを取りながら野菜類が
柔らかくなるまで煮込む。

7　しょうゆを加え、中火で煮汁が
なくなるまでいりつけ、ピーマンを加えて
さっと煮て、火をとめる。

Chicken and Vegetables, *Chikuzen*-style

Chikuzen-ni

230 kcal per serving

◆ DIRECTIONS

1 Cut chicken into bite-sized pieces.

2 Cut carrot, burdock, and lotus root into rolling wedges, trim stems off *shiitake*, and cut the caps into quarters.

3 Cut bell peppers lengthwise into quarters, remove stems and seeds, and slice into ³⁄₈-inch strips.

4 Tear *konnyaku* into bite-sized pieces by hand, parboil briefly.

5 Heat oil in a skillet, add chicken, carrot, burdock, lotus root, *konnyaku*, and *shiitake* in order, and stir-fry.

6 Add *dashi*, sugar, and *mirin*, and cover with a drop-lid. Bring to a boil, then lower heat. Cook until vegetables are tender, skimming.

7 Add soy sauce and keep cooking over medium heat until the sauce is almost gone. Add bell pepper, and cook briefly. Remove from heat.

◆ INGREDIENTS (4 servings)

14 oz chicken thighs, boned
1 (5¹⁄₄ oz) carrot
1 (3¹⁄₂ oz) burdock root
2-inch (3¹⁄₂ oz) lotus root
4 fresh *shiitake* mushrooms
2 green bell peppers
¹⁄₂ cake (4¹⁄₂ oz) *konnyaku* (devil's tongue jelly)
vegetable oil
Sauce

- 2¹⁄₂ U.S. cups *dashi*
- 2 Tbsp sugar
- 3 Tbsp *mirin*
- 5 Tbsp soy sauce

めばるの煮つけ

1人分 190 kcal

◆材　料 (4人分)

めばる (200 gのもの)　4尾
煮汁
　酒　400 cc
　水　200 cc
　砂糖　大さじ3
　みりん　大さじ4
　しょうゆ　大さじ7
しょうが (薄切り)　30 g
木綿豆腐　1丁 (300 g)
木の芽　適量

◆作り方

1 めばるはうろこを包丁でこそげとり、
えらを取る。腹に切り込みを入れ、
内臓を取り出す。(魚屋でやってもらえる)。
水できれいに洗う。→**❶❷**

2 ボールにめばるを入れて、80℃の湯を
注ぎ、うっすらと白くなったら、水にとり、
ぬめりや残っているうろこを落とす。

3 鍋に煮汁の材料としょうがの薄切りを
煮立て、めばるを並べて入れ、
落としぶたをして強火で一気に
5〜6分煮る。→**❸**

4 豆腐は3cm角に切り、**3**の鍋に加えて
2分煮る。

5 器に盛り、煮汁をかけて木の芽を
のせる。

メ モ
• 魚の煮つけは必ず煮汁が煮立ったところに
入れること。
• かれい、さば、あじ、金目だい、さわらなどで
もおいしい。

❶

❷

❸

Simmered Rockfish

Mebaru no Nitsuke

190 kcal per serving

◆ DIRECTIONS

1　Scale fish on both sides with a knife, and remove gills. Slit belly, remove entrails. You can also have the fish cleaned at the store. Wash well with cold water. →❶❷

2　Place the fish in a bowl with hot water (180°F) to cover the fish. When skin whitens, plunge in cold water and remove any remaining debris.

3　Combine all sauce ingredients and slivered ginger in a skillet, and bring to a boil. Distribute the fish evenly in the skillet, cover with a drop lid, and cook 5–6 minutes over high heat.→❸

4　Cut tofu into 1-inch cubes, add to the skillet, and cook for 2 minetes.

5　Transfer the fish to serving dishes, pour sauce over, and top with *kinome* sprigs.

NOTES
• Simmered fish: Be sure to add the fish to sauce that is boiling.
• This cooking method is also good for halibut, mackerel, horse mackerel, red snapper, and Spanish mackerel.

◆ INGREDIENTS (4 servings)

4 rockfish, 7 oz each
Sauce
⎧ 1²⁄₃ U.S. cups *saké*
⎪ 6²⁄₃ oz water
⎨ 3 Tbsp sugar
⎪ 4 Tbsp *mirin*
⎩ 7 Tbsp soy sauce
1 oz fresh ginger, finely slivered
1 cake (10¹⁄₂ oz) "cotton" tofu
kinome sprigs

さばのみそ煮

| 1人分 330 kcal |

◆材　料(4人分)

さば(上身100 g)　4切れ
しょうが　30 g
青ねぎ　4本
煮汁
　酒　100 cc
　水　100 cc
　砂糖　大さじ3
　赤みそ　80 g

◆作り方

1　さばは皮に2〜3本斜めに切り目を入れる。→❶

2　ボールに入れて、80℃の湯を注ぎ、臭みを取る。

3　しょうがは薄切りに、青ねぎは3cm長さに切る。

4　鍋にさば、しょうが、酒、水を入れ、落としぶたをして強火にかけ、煮立ったらアクを取り、中火にしてさばに火を通す。

5　弱火にして砂糖、煮汁少々で溶きのばしたみそを加え、さらに5分ほど煮る。→❷

6　青ねぎを加え、さっと煮て火をとめる。

7　器に盛り、煮汁をかける。

❶

❷

Simmered Mackerel in Miso

Saba no Miso-ni

330 kcal per serving

◆ DIRECTIONS

1 Score the skin of the fish diagonally in several places.→❶

2 Place the fish in a bowl, and pour hot water (180°F) over it to remove the fishy odor.

3 Cut ginger into thin slices, and scallions into 1-inch lengths.

4 Place mackerel, ginger, *saké*, and water in a skillet, cover with a drop-lid, and set over high heat. When it boils, skim and lower the heat to medium, then cook until fish is done.

5 Lower heat, add sugar and miso dissolved with a little cooking sauce in the skillet, and cook 5 more minutes.→❷

6 Add scallions, cook briefly, and remove from heat.

7 Arrange in serving bowls, pour sauce over, and serve.

◆ INGREDIENTS (4 servings)

4 mackerel fillets,
    3 1/2 oz each
1 oz fresh ginger
4 scallions
Sauce
    3 1/3 oz *saké*
    3 1/3 oz water
    3 Tbsp sugar
    2 4/5 oz red miso

豚角煮

1人分 710 kcal

◆材 料(4人分)

豚ばら肉 (ブロック) 600 g
サラダ油 適量
しょうが (薄切り) 50 g
煮汁
 だし 400 cc
 酒 200 cc
 砂糖 大さじ3
 みりん 50 cc
 しょうゆ 100 cc
小玉ねぎ 12個
グリーンピース (水煮)
 大さじ4
練りがらし 適量

◆作り方

1 豚ばら肉は6cm角に切り、フライパンに油を熱し、豚肉全面に焼き色をつける。→❶

2 豚肉をたっぷりの水で約1時間下ゆでする。

3 鍋に豚肉をすき間なく詰め、しょうが、酒、だしを入れ、落としぶたをして中火で10〜15分煮る。残りの調味料を加え、弱火で30分煮込む。火をとめてそのまま完全にさます。→❷

4 小玉ねぎは熱湯で3分ゆでる。

5 食べる前に再び火にかけ、小玉ねぎを加えて軽く煮込み、仕上げにグリーンピースを加える。

6 器に盛り、煮汁をかけて、からしを添える。

Braised Pork, Nagasaki-style

Buta Kaku-ni

```
710 kcal per serving
```

◆ DIRECTIONS

1 Cut pork belly into 2½-inch cubes. Heat oil in a skillet, and brown pork evenly.→❶

2 Boil pork in ample water for about 1 hour.

3 Place pork neatly in a skillet with ginger, *dashi* and *saké*, and cover with a drop-lid. Cook over medium heat for 10–15 minutes. Add the remaining seasonings, and cook over low heat for 30 minutes. Remove from heat and let stand until cooled completely.→❷

4 Parboil pearl onions in water for 3 minutes.

5 Reheat the skillet before serving, add pearl onions, and simmer lightly. Sprinkle with green peas.

6 Transfer into serving bowls, pour sauce over, and serve with mustard.

◆ INGREDIENTS (4 servings)

21 oz boneless pork belly
vegetable oil
1¾ oz fresh ginger, thinly sliced
Sauce
  ⎰ 1⅔ U.S. cups *dashi*
  ⎱ 6⅔ oz *saké*
  ⎰ 3 Tbsp sugar
  ⎱ 1⅔ oz *mirin*
  ⎰ 3⅓ oz soy sauce
12 pearl onions
4 Tbsp parboiled green peas
mustard

❶

❷

鶏の治部煮

1人分 260 kcal

◆材　料 (4人分)

鶏もも肉 (または合鴨胸肉)
　1枚 (400 g)
片栗粉　適量
長ねぎ　1本
煮汁
　┌ だし　200 cc
　│ 酒　100 cc
　┤ 砂糖　大さじ1
　│ みりん　大さじ4
　└ しょうゆ　大さじ4
おろしわさび (→116頁)
　小さじ1

◆作り方

1　鶏肉は皮を下にして斜めに
そぎ切りにする。片栗粉をまぶし、
余分な粉は払い落とす。→❶

2　長ねぎは斜め切りにする。→❷

3　鍋に煮汁の材料を入れて一煮立ち
させ、鶏肉を入れ、表裏を返しながら
5〜6分煮て火を通す。

4　長ねぎを加え、さっと煮て、仕上げに
わさびを入れて火をとめる。

メモ
•治部煮は鴨肉に小麦粉や片栗粉をまぶして
煮る金沢の郷土料理。

❶

❷

Chicken, *Jibu-ni*-style

Tori no Jibu-ni

260 kcal per serving

◆ DIRECTIONS

1 Place the chicken on a cutting board with skin side down. Slice chicken diagonally into strips. Pat with cornstarch, and discard any excess starch. →❶

2 Slice Japanese leek diagonally. →❷

3 Combine all sauce ingredients in a skillet, bring to a boil, add chicken, and cook for 5–6 minutes turning the meat.

4 Add leek, cook briefly, add grated *wasabi*, and remove from heat.

NOTE
• *Jibu-ni* is a dish from the Kanazawa region, using duck that has been dusted with flour or cornstarch and simmered.

◆ INGREDIENTS (4 servings)

14 oz chicken thighs
　or duck breast
cornstarch
1 Japanese leek
Sauce
⎰ 6²/₃ oz *dashi*
⎥ 3¹/₃ oz *saké*
⎥ 1 Tbsp sugar
⎥ 4 Tbsp *mirin*
⎱ 4 Tbsp soy sauce
1 tsp grated *wasabi*
　horseradish (→p. 117)

牛肉と野菜の旨煮

1人分　230 kcal

◆材 料(4人分)

牛ヒレ肉　200 g
たけのこ (水煮)　200 g
にんじん　½本 (100 g)
かぼちゃ　⅙個 (200 g)
生しいたけ　4枚
しょうが　20 g
さやいんげん　4本
塩　少々
サラダ油　大さじ2
煮汁
　だし　500 cc
　酒　100 cc
　砂糖　大さじ3
　みりん　大さじ1
　薄口しょうゆ　大さじ4

◆作り方

1　牛肉、たけのこは3cm角に切る。
にんじん、かぼちゃは皮をむいて、
同様にする。しいたけは軸を取り、
四つ切りにする。しょうがはせん切りに
する。

2　さやいんげんは塩ゆでし、3cm長さに
切る。

3　鍋に油を熱して、牛肉、しょうがを
いためる。焼き色がついたら、にんじん、
かぼちゃ、たけのこ、しいたけの順に
入れてよくいため、だし、酒を加えて
中火で約20分煮る。

4　砂糖、みりん、薄口しょうゆを加え、
さらに15分煮る。

5　さやいんげんを加え、火をとめる。

Simmered Beef with Vegetables

Gyūniku to Yasai no Uma-ni

230 kcal per serving

◆ DIRECTIONS

1   Peel carrot and squash. Cut beef, bamboo shoots, carrot, and squash into 1-inch cubes. Trim mushroom stems and quarter the caps. Slice ginger into fine slivers.

2   Parboil green beans in lightly salted water, and cut into 1-inch lengths.

3   Heat oil in a skillet, and stir-fry beef and ginger. When meat is brown, add carrot, squash, bamboo shoots, and *shiitake* in order, and sauté well. Add *dashi* and *saké*, and simmer over medium heat for 20 minutes.

4   Add sugar, *mirin*, and light soy sauce, and cook 15 minutes.

5   Add green beans, and remove from heat.

◆ INGREDIENTS (4 servings)

7 oz beef tenderloin
7 oz boiled bamboo shoots
1/2 (3 1/2 oz) carrot
1/6 (7 oz) acorn squash
4 fresh *shiitake* mushrooms
2/3 oz fresh ginger
4 green beans
pinch salt
2 Tbsp vegetable oil
Sauce
   2 1/8 U.S. cups *dashi*
   3 1/3 oz *saké*
   3 Tbsp sugar
   1 Tbsp *mirin*
   4 Tbsp light soy sauce

牛肉のアスパラガス巻き

1人分 230 kcal

◆材料(4人分)

グリーンアスパラガス　4本
塩　少々
牛ロース肉 (薄切り)　300 g
サラダ油　適量
たれ
  酒　100 cc
  砂糖　大さじ2
  みりん　大さじ3
  しょうゆ　大さじ5
練りがらし　適量

◆作り方

1　グリーンアスパラガスは根元を
たわめてみて、ポキッと折れるところで折
り、下の方のかたい皮をむいて、塩ゆで
にし、縦に四つ割りにする。

2　牛肉を広げ、アスパラガスを巻く。→❶

3　フライパンに油を熱し、強火で全体に
焼き色をつけ、一度取り出す。

4　そのフライパンにたれの材料を入れて
煮つめ、牛肉をもどし、たれをからめる。

5　熱いうちに1cm幅に切り、器に盛り、
からしを添える。

❶

Rolled Beef and Asparagus

Gyūniku no Asuparagasu-maki

230 kcal per serving

◆ DIRECTIONS

1 Break off the tough ends and peel the lower part of asparagus, parboil in salted water, and cut into quarters lengthwise.

2 Spread beef slices, distribute asparagus evenly, and roll beef around asparagus as a core. →❶

3 Heat oil in a frying pan, brown the rolls, and remove from pan.

4 Combine all sauce ingredients in the frying pan, and cook down. Return the beef rolls to the pan, and shake to coat evenly.

5 Cut rolls into ⅜-inch pieces, and arrange in a serving dish. Serve with mustard.

◆ INGREDIENTS (4 servings)

4 stalks green asparagus
pinch salt
10½ oz beef sirloin,
    thinly sliced
vegetable oil
Sauce
    ⎡ 3⅓ oz *saké*
    ⎢ 2 Tbsp sugar
    ⎢ 3 Tbsp *mirin*
    ⎣ 5 Tbsp soy sauce
mustard

てんぷら

1人分 540 kcal

◆材 料(4人分)

えび(殻つき、無頭) 8尾
いか(上身) 100 g
きす(上身、皮つき) 4尾
生しいたけ 4枚
かぼちゃ 100 g
さつま芋 100 g
ピーマン 2個
野菜のかき揚げ
　さつま芋 150 g
　玉ねぎ ½個(70 g)
　三つ葉 1束(50 g)
衣
　卵黄1個＋冷水 1カップ
　小麦粉 1カップ
てんつゆ
　だし 1½カップ
　みりん 大さじ4
　しょうゆ 大さじ4
薬味
　大根おろし 大さじ6
　おろししょうが 小さじ2
　レモンのくし形切り 適量
　塩 適量
小麦粉 適量
揚げ油 適量

◆作り方

1 てんつゆを作る。鍋にみりんを煮立て(煮きりみりん)、だし、しょうゆを加えて、再び煮立ったら火をとめる。

2 えびは背わたを取り、尾を残して殻をむく。尾先を切り、包丁の先でしごいて水を出す。腹に切り込みを数ヵ所入れ、押さえるようにして筋をのばす(62頁参照)。

3 いかは薄皮をむき、表面に縦横に切り込みを入れ、一口大に切る。→❶

4 えび、いか、きすの水けをふき取る。

5 しいたけは軸を取る。かぼちゃ、さつま芋は薄く切る。ピーマンは縦4つに切り、へた、種を取る。

6 かき揚げの材料のさつま芋はマッチ棒の大きさに、玉ねぎは薄切りに、三つ葉は3cm長さに切り、ボールに合わせ、小麦粉を薄くふる。

7 衣を作る。ボールに卵黄と冷水を混ぜ合わせ、小麦粉をさっくり混ぜる*。→❷

*衣は混ぜすぎたり、水が生ぬるいと粘りが出て、カラリと揚がらない。衣は低温に保つこと。

❶

❷

Tempura

540 kcal per serving

◆ DIRECTIONS

1 To make dipping sauce, bring *mirin* to boil, then add *dashi* and soy sauce. When it boils for the second time, remove from heat.

2 Devein shrimp, and shell, leaving the tail intact. Trim tail of shrimp by cutting off tip, and force out any moisture with the dull edge of a knife. Make several shallow cuts across the underside of each shrimp so that they lie flat. See page 62.

3 Skin squid, score each side in a shallow diamond pattern, cut into bite-sized pieces. →❶

4 Pat dry shrimp, squid, and sillago.

5 Trim stems off *shiitake*. Cut acorn squash and sweet potato into thin slices. Cut bell peppers into quarters lengthwise, remove stems and seeds.

6 For mixed vegetable tempura, julienne sweet potato, slice onion thinly, cut *mitsuba* into 1-inch lengths. Mix vegetables in a bowl, and sprinkle with flour.

7 To make batter, mix egg yolk and ice water in a bowl, add flour, and mix lightly.*→❷

*If overbeaten, or if the water is not cold enough, the batter becomes somewhat sticky, and will not produce a crispy finish when fried. Be sure to keep the batter chilled.

◆ INGREDIENTS (4 servings)

8 shrimp in shells
   without heads
3 1/2 oz squid (body only)
4 sillago fillets with skin
4 fresh *shiitake* mushrooms
3 1/2 oz acorn squash
3 1/2 oz sweet potato
2 green bell peppers
Mixed Vegetable Tempura
   5 1/4 oz sweet potato
   1/2 (2 1/2 oz) onion
   1 bunch (1 3/4 oz)
      mitsuba (trefoil)
Batter
   1 egg yolk + ice water
      to make 1 cup
   1 cup flour
Dipping Sauce
   10 oz *dashi*
   4 Tbsp *mirin*
   4 Tbsp soy sauce
Condiments
   6 Tbsp grated
      daikon radish
   2 tsp grated fresh ginger
   lemon wedges
   salt
flour
oil for deep-frying

❸

8 165〜170℃の揚げ油で野菜類、175℃に上げて魚介類を、それぞれに小麦粉をまぶし、衣をつけながら揚げる。→❸

9 残りの衣をかき揚げの材料に入れてからませ、170℃の油に1/4量を滑り込ませるように入れて形作り、カラリと揚げる。→❹

10 揚げたてを盛り合わせ、てんつゆ、薬味、塩を添え、好みの味で食べる。かき揚げは、てんつゆがよい。

❹

• 揚げ油の温度の見分け方
衣を1滴落としてみる。
約160℃＝いったん底まで沈み、ゆっくり上がってくる。

• **To determine oil temperature**
320°F=A drop of batter will sink to the bottom of the pan, and slowly float up to the surface.

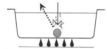

約170℃＝途中まで沈んで、浮き上がる。

340°F=A drop of batter will sink halfway to the bottom, and float up.

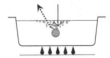

約180℃＝表面近くで音をたてて浮く。

360°F=A drop of batter will float on the surface, making a frying sound.

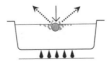

8 Preheat oil to 330–340°F. Dust ingredients with flour, dip each vegetable in batter, and deep-fry. Do the same with fish at higher temperature (350°F). →❸

9 Add the remaining batter to the bowl of mixed vegetables, mix well, and slip ¼ of the mixture at a time into oil at 340°F. Deep-fry until crispy. →❹

10 Arrange hot food on serving plates, and serve with dipping sauce, condiments, and salt to taste. Dipping sauce is recommended for mixed vegetable tempura.

鶏の竜田揚げ

| 1人分 370 kcal |

◆材　料(4人分)

鶏もも肉 (骨なし)
　1枚 (400 g)
ピーマン (赤、緑) 各1個
漬け汁
　┌ 酒　大さじ2
　│ みりん　大さじ2
　│ しょうゆ　大さじ2
　└ しょうがの絞り汁　小さじ1
衣
　┌ 卵白　2個分
　│ 片栗粉　大さじ3
　│ 青ねぎ (みじん切り)
　│ 　大さじ2
　│ しょうが (みじん切り)
　└ 　大さじ1
片栗粉　適量
揚げ油　適量
レモンのくし形切り　4個

◆作り方

1 鶏肉は3cm角に切り、漬け汁に
30分つける。

2 ピーマンは縦半分に
切り、種を取り、もみじ
形に切り抜く。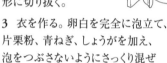

3 衣を作る。卵白を完全に泡立て、
片栗粉、青ねぎ、しょうがを加え、
泡をつぶさないようにさっくり混ぜ
合わせる。

4 鶏肉の汁けをふき取り、片栗粉を
薄くまぶし、余分な粉は払い落とす。

5 揚げ油を165〜170℃に熱し、鶏肉に**3**
の衣をたっぷりつけて色よく揚げる。→**❶❷**

6 もみじ形に抜いたピーマンを165℃の
揚げ油でさっと揚げる。

7 器に盛りつけ、レモンを添える。

❶

❷

Deep-Fried Marinated Chicken

Tori no Tatsuta-age

370 kcal per serving

◆ DIRECTIONS

1 Cut chicken into 1-inch cubes. Marinate chicken in seasoning sauce for 30 minutes.

2 Cut bell peppers in half lengthwise, remove seeds, and cut into maple leaf shapes.

3 To make batter, beat egg whites until frothy, add cornstarch, scallions, ginger, and mix lightly.

4 Pat chicken dry, dust with cornstarch, and shake off excess.

5 Preheat oil to 330–340°F. Coat chicken well with batter, and deep-fry until brown. →❶❷

6 Deep-fry peppers briefly at 330°F.

7 Arrange chicken and peppers on serving plates, garnish with lemon wedges.

◆ INGREDIENTS (4 servings)

14 oz chicken thighs, boned
1 red bell pepper
1 green bell pepper

Seasoning Sauce
- 2 Tbsp *saké*
- 2 Tbsp *mirin*
- 2 Tbsp soy sauce
- 1 tsp fresh ginger juice

Batter
- 2 egg whites
- 3 Tbsp cornstarch
- 2 Tbsp finely chopped scallions
- 1 Tbsp finely chopped fresh ginger

cornstarch
oil for deep-frying
4 lemon wedges

とんカツ

1人分 500 kcal

◆材　料 (4人分)

豚ロース肉 (120 gのもの)
　4枚
塩、こしょう　各適量
衣
　- 小麦粉　適量
　- 溶き卵　1個分
　- パン粉　適量
ソース
　- ウスターソース　大さじ6
　- トマトケチャップ　大さじ4
　- しょうゆ　大さじ3
キャベツ (せん切り)　100 g
ラディッシュ　4個
レモンのくし形切り　4個
練りがらし　適量
揚げ油　適量

◆作り方

1　豚肉は脂身と赤身の間の筋を
数ヵ所切り、両面に塩、こしょうをふる。→❶

2　小麦粉を薄くまぶし、溶き卵、パン粉
の順につける。パン粉は手で軽く押さえ
て、落ちつかせる。

3　160℃の揚げ油に肉をすべり込ませ、
片側に揚げ色がついたら返して、
少しずつ温度を上げ (180℃) カラッと
揚げる。

4　油をきって、食べやすい大きさに切る。

5　ソースの材料を混ぜ合わせる。

6　キャベツ、ラディッシュをつけ合わせ、
ソース、レモン、練りがらしを添える。

❶

Pork Cutlets

Tonkatsu

500 kcal per serving

◆ DIRECTIONS

1   To dress pork, cut stringy membrane between fat and meat in several places, and sprinkle salt and pepper on both sides. →❶

2   Dust pork lightly with flour, dip in beaten egg, and bread. Secure bread crumbs by patting.

3   Slide pork into 320°F oil, turn over when brown, raise oil to 360°F, and deep-fry until crispy.

4   Remove excess oil by draining on paper towels, and cut into bite-sized pieces.

5   Mix all sauce ingredients.

6   Garnish with shredded cabbage and radishes, and serve with sauce, lemon, and mustard.

◆ INGREDIENTS (4 servings)

4 pork loin cuts,
  4¹/₅ oz each
salt and pepper
Breading
  { flour
  { 1 egg, beaten
  { bread crumbs
Sauce
  { 6 Tbsp Worcestershire
  {   sauce
  { 4 Tbsp tomato ketchup
  { 3 Tbsp soy sauce
3¹/₂ oz cabbage, shredded
4 red radishes
4 lemon wedges
mustard
oil for deep-frying

串揚げ

1人分 870 kcal

◆材 料(4人分)

A 牛ヒレ肉　100 g
　ピーマン　1個

B 牛ロース肉 (薄切り)
　　　100 g
　グリーンアスパラガス
　　　4本

C 豚ロース肉 (薄切り)
　　　100 g
　グリュイエルチーズ　50 g

D 鶏もも肉　100 g
　長ねぎ　1本

E いか　100 g
　のり　1/4枚

F 白身魚　120 g

G 帆立て貝の貝柱
　　　4個 (200 g)

H えび (殻つき、無頭)
　　　4尾

衣
[卵黄2個＋冷水　2カップ
小麦粉＋ベーキングパウダー
　小さじ1/2　2カップ]

小麦粉、パン粉　各適量

揚げ油　適量

ソース (→192頁)　200 cc

レモンのくし形切り　4個

粒マスタード　適量

塩　適量

つけ野菜
[青ねぎ、にんじん、セロリ、
きゅうり　各適量]

◆作り方

1　A=牛ヒレ肉、ピーマンを2cm角に切って交互に串に刺す。B=アスパラガスは根元のかたい部分の皮をむき、牛肉で巻いて、3cm長さに切り、串に刺す。C=チーズは1cm角の2cm長さの棒状に切り、豚肉で巻いて串に刺す。D=鶏肉は2cm角に、長ねぎは2cm長さに切り、交互に串に刺す。E=いかは2cm角に切り、2cm幅ののりで巻き、串に刺す。F=白身魚は一口大に切って、串に刺す。G=貝柱は半分に切り、1個分を串に刺す。H=えびは背わたを取り、尾を残して殻をむき、串を刺す。

2　つけ野菜の青ねぎは5cm長さに切り、にんじん、セロリ、きゅうりは1cm角5cm長さの棒状にする。

3　衣を作る。ボールに卵黄と冷水を混ぜ合わせ、小麦粉、ベーキングパウダーをさっくり混ぜる。

4　それぞれの串に小麦粉、衣、パン粉の順につけ、170℃の揚げ油で揚げる。

5　串揚げを盛り、ソース、レモン、マスタード、塩、つけ野菜を添える。

Deep-Fried Mixed Kebabs
Kushi-age

870 kcal per serving

◆ DIRECTIONS

1 **A**=Cut beef and bell pepper into
³/₄-inch cubes, and thread 2–3 pieces to a
skewer, alternating beef and pepper.
B=Peel the tough part of asparagus, wrap
in beef, cut rolls into 1-inch lengths, and
skewer. **C**=Cut cheese into ³/₈ × ³/₈ × ³/₄-
inch sticks, wrap in pork, and skewer.
D=Cut chicken into ³/₄-inch cubes, cut
Japanese leek into ³/₄-inch lengths, and
skewer, alternating. **E**=Cut squid into ³/₄-
inch squares, wrap with *nori* seaweed of
the same size, and skewer. **F**=Cut fish
into bite-sized pieces, and skewer.
G=Cut scallops in half, and thread 2
pieces per skewer. **H**=Shell and devein
shrimp leaving tails, and skewer.

2 Cut scallions into 2-inch lengths, and
carrots, celery, and cucumber
into ³/₈ × ³/₈ × 2-inch sticks.

3 To make batter, mix egg yolks
and ice water and stir. Add flour
and baking powder, mix lightly.

4 Dust each skewer with flour, dip in
batter, and roll in bread
crumbs. Deep-fry at
340°F.

5 Arrange the
skewers, garnish-
ing with raw
vegetables. Serve
with sauce,
lemon, mustard,
and salt to taste.

◆ INGREDIENTS (4 servings)

A 3¹/₂ oz beef tenderloin
   1 green bell pepper
B 3¹/₂ oz beef loin,
   thinly sliced
   4 stalks green asparagus
C 3¹/₂ oz pork loin,
   thinly sliced
   1³/₄ oz Gruyère cheese
D 3¹/₂ oz chicken thighs
   1 Japanese leek
E 3¹/₂ oz squid
   ¹/₄ sheet *nori* seaweed
F 4¹/₅ oz white-fleshed
   fish fillet
G 4 (7 oz) shucked
   scallops
H 4 shrimp in shells
   without heads

Batter
⎧ 2 egg yolks + ice water
⎪   to make 2 cups
⎨ flour + ¹/₂ tsp baking
⎪   powder to make
⎩   2 cups

flour and bread crumbs
oil for deep-frying
6²/₃ oz sauce (→p. 193)
4 lemon wedges
stone-ground mustard
salt

Garnish
⎧ scallions, carrots, celery,
⎨ cucumbers

かれいのから揚げ

| 1人分 290 kcal |

◆**材　料**(4人分)

かれい (200 gのもの)　4尾
しし唐　8本
春雨　10 g
ポン酢 (市販品でも可)
　柑橘類の絞り汁　50 cc
　しょうゆ　150 cc
さらしねぎ　大さじ4
大根おろし　大さじ4
レモンのくし形切り　4個
塩　大さじ2
小麦粉　適量
揚げ油　適量

◆**作り方**

1　かれいはうろこを包丁でこそげとり、腹に切り込みを入れ、えらと内臓を取り出す(魚屋でやってもらえる)。水でよく洗い、頭をつけたまま表身から2枚、裏身から2枚、中骨1枚の五枚におろす。身は3つに切り分ける。身と中骨に小麦粉を薄くまぶす。→❶

2　しし唐はへたを落とし、切り込みを入れ、種を取る。

3　揚げ油を165℃に熱し、中骨を入れ、箸で押さえながら水分を抜くようにじっくりと揚げる。身は油を170℃に上げて、こんがりと揚げる。→❷

4　しし唐は170℃の油で素揚げする。

5　春雨は170℃の油にパッと入れ、浮き上がってきたらすぐに紙の上に取り出し、砕く。

6　器に盛りつけ、ポン酢にさらしねぎと大根おろしを加えたもの、レモン、塩を添える。

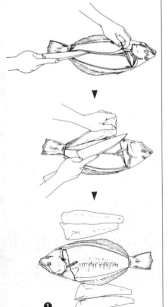

❶

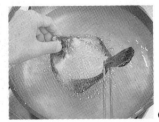

❷

Deep-Fried Flounder Boat

Karei no Kara-age

290 kcal per serving

◆ DIRECTIONS

1 Scale flounder with back of a knife, slit belly, and remove gills and entrails. (You can also have them cleaned at the store.) Rinse well with water, and fillet, making 2 pieces from each side, reserving the bones, heads and tails. Cut each fillet into 3 pieces. Dust flour lightly on fish and bones. →❶

2 Cut stems off green peppers, slit lengthwise, and remove seeds.

3 Preheat oil to 330°F. Place bones in the pan, and deep-fry slowly to remove moisture, holding with chopsticks. Heat up oil to 340°F, and deep-fry fillets until crispy. →❷

4 Deep-fry green pepper at 340°F.

5 Drop *harusame* noodles in oil at 340°F. As soon as they puff up and float, remove from oil, place on paper towels, and crumble.

6 Arrange fillets on top of bones, serve with lemon-soy sauce, rinsed scallions, grated *daikon* radish, and lemon seasoned with salt.

◆ INGREDIENTS (4 servings)

4 flounder, 7 oz each
8 small sweet green
  peppers
1/3 oz *harusame*
  (saifun noodles)
Lemon-Soy Sauce
  (or *Ponzu*)
  { 1 2/3 oz lemon juice
  { 5 oz soy sauce
4 Tbsp rinsed scallions
4 Tbsp grated *daikon*
  radish
4 lemon wedges
2 Tbsp salt
flour
oil for deep-frying

揚げだし豆腐

1人分 200 kcal

◆材　料(4人分)

絹ごし豆腐 (100 gのもの)
　4個

べっこうあん

　だし　300 cc
　砂糖　大さじ1
　みりん　大さじ4
　しょうゆ　大さじ5
　水溶き片栗粉
　　片栗粉　大さじ3
　　水　大さじ3

薬味

　さらしねぎ (→32頁)
　　大さじ2
　おろししょうが　大さじ1
　糸花がつお　適量

小麦粉　適量
揚げ油　適量

◆作り方

1 豆腐は布巾やペーパータオルに包み、斜めにしたまな板にのせ、軽く重石をし、30分おいて水けをきる。→❶

2 鍋にべっこうあんのだしと調味料を入れて煮立たせ、水溶き片栗粉を加えてとろみをつける。→❷

3 豆腐の水けをふき取り、小麦粉を薄く全体にまぶす。

4 揚げ油を170〜175℃に熱し、豆腐をこんがり揚げる。→❸

5 器に揚げたての豆腐を盛ってあんをかけ、さらしねぎ、おろししょうが、糸花がつおをのせる。

❶

❷

❸

Deep-Fried Tofu with Amber Sauce

Agedashi-dōfu

200 kcal per serving

◆ DIRECTIONS

1 Wrap tofu cakes in cheesecloth or paper towels, and place on a tilted cutting board. Weight lightly on top and let stand for 30 minutes to remove excess water. →❶

2 Combine *dashi* and seasonings for sauce in a soup pan, bring to a boil, and add starch-water mixture to thicken. →❷

3 Pat tofu dry, and dust lightly with flour.

4 Preheat oil to 340–350°F, and deep-fry tofu until golden brown. →❸

5 Transfer hot tofu to small bowls, pour amber sauce over, top with bonito threads, and mound scallions and grated ginger alongside.

◆ INGREDIENTS (4 servings)

4 cakes "silken" tofu, 3 1/2 oz each

Amber Sauce
- 10 oz *dashi*
- 1 Tbsp sugar
- 4 Tbsp *mirin*
- 5 Tbsp soy sauce
- starch-water mixture
  - 3 Tbsp cornstarch
  - 3 Tbsp water

Condiments
- 2 Tbsp rinsed scallions (→p. 33)
- 1 Tbsp grated fresh ginger
- dried bonito threads

flour

oil for deep-frying

なすのはさみ揚げ

1人分 240 kcal

◆材　料(4人分)

米なす　1個(200 g)
鶏ひき肉　150 g
卵　½個
片栗粉　大さじ1
塩　少々
てんつゆ
[
  だし　300 cc
  みりん　大さじ4
  しょうゆ　大さじ4
]
薬味
[
  さらしねぎ(→32頁)
  大根おろし
  おろししょうが
  　各適量
]
小麦粉　適量
揚げ油　適量

◆作り方

1　てんつゆを作る。鍋にみりんを煮立て(煮きりみりん)、だし、しょうゆを加えて、煮立ったら火をとめる。

2　なすはへたを切り落として縦に皮をむく。四つ割りにし、1cm厚さに切り、水にさらす。

3　ボールにひき肉、卵、片栗粉、塩を混ぜ合わせて練る。

4　なすの水けをよくふき取り、全体に小麦粉を薄くまぶし、肉をはさむ。→❶

5　揚げ油を170℃に熱して、こんがりと揚げる。

6　器に盛り、てんつゆ、薬味を添える。

Deep-Fried Eggplant Sandwiches

Nasu no Hasami-age

240 kcal per serving

◆ DIRECTIONS

1 To make dipping sauce, boil *mirin* in a saucepan ("*nikiri-mirin*"), add *dashi*, soy sauce, and remove from heat when it boils for the second time.

2 Peel eggplant skin from top to bottom. Cut eggplant into quarters, slice into ⅜-inch thick slices, and soak in water.

3 Combine ground chicken, egg, cornstarch, and salt in a bowl, and mix well, kneading.

4 Pat eggplant slices dry, dust lightly with flour, and make sandwiches with ground chicken filling.→❶

5 Preheat oil to 340°F. Deep-fry sandwiches until golden brown.

6 Mound sandwiches in small bowls, serve with dipping sauce and condiments on the side.

◆ INGREDIENTS (4 servings)

1 (7 oz) American eggplant
5¼ oz ground chicken
½ lightly beaten egg
1 Tbsp cornstarch
pinch salt
Dipping Sauce
⎰ 10 oz *dashi*
⎱ 4 Tbsp *mirin*
  4 Tbsp soy sauce
Condiments
⎰ rinsed scallions
⎱   (→p. 33)
  grated *daikon* radish
  grated fresh ginger
flour
oil for deep-frying

❶

えびのコーンフレーク揚げ

1人分 180 kcal

◆材　料(4人分)

えび (無頭)　12尾
卵　1個
コーンフレーク (無糖)　適量
小麦粉　適量
揚げ油　適量
レモンのくし形切り　4個
塩　適量

◆作り方

1　えびは背わたを取り、尾を残し殻を
むく。尾先を切り、包丁の先でしごいて
水を出す。腹に数ヵ所切り目を入れて
まっすぐにのばす。62頁参照。

2　卵は溶きほぐす。コーンフレークは
粗く砕く。

3　えびに小麦粉を薄くまぶし、溶き卵、
コーンフレークの順につける。→❶

4　揚げ油を170℃に熱し、揚げる。→❷

5　器に盛り、レモン、塩を添える。

応用
• コーンフレークの代わりに、ピスタチオ、
白ごまなどでもよい。

❶

❷

Deep-Fried Shrimp with Cornflake Batter

Ebi no Kōnfurēku-age

180 kcal per serving

◆ DIRECTIONS

1   Devein shrimp, and shell, leaving tails. Cut off the tip of tails, and force out any moisture with the back of a knife. Score underside of shrimp at several places to flatten. See page 62.

2   Beat egg lightly. Crumble cornflakes.

3   Dust shrimp lightly with flour, dip in beaten egg, and coat with crumbled cornflakes.→❶

4   Preheat oil to 340°F, and deep-fry shrimp.→❷

5   Arrange shrimp on plates, and serve with lemon wedges and salt.

NOTE
• Pistachio nuts or white sesame seeds can also be used for coating.

◆ INGREDIENTS (4 servings)

12 shrimp in shells
   without heads
1 egg
plain cornflakes
flour
oil for deep-frying
4 lemon wedges
salt

いわしの薩摩揚げ

1人分 320 kcal

◆材　料(4人分)

いわし　600g
片栗粉　大さじ2
塩　小さじ½
しょうゆ　小さじ1
卵　1個
しょうが (みじん切り)
　　大さじ1
青ねぎ (みじん切り)
　　大さじ1
大根おろし　大さじ6
しょうゆ　適量
揚げ油　適量

◆作り方

1　いわしは頭と内臓、骨を取る。
流水でよく洗って、皮を取り、水けを
ふき取る。

2　いわしは細かく刻んで、すり鉢に移し、
片栗粉、塩、しょうゆを加えて、よくする。
粘りが出てきたら、卵を加え、
よく練り混ぜる。しょうが、青ねぎを加えて
混ぜ合わせる(フードプロセッサーを使っ
てもよい)。

3　揚げ油を170〜175℃に熱し、小さじで
すくって形作りながら入れ、キツネ色に
カラッと揚げる。→❶

4　器に盛り、大根おろしをのせ、
しょうゆをかける。

❶

Deep-Fried Sardine Balls

Iwashi no Satsuma-age

320 kcal per serving

◆ DIRECTIONS

1   Remove heads, entrails, and bones of sardines. Rinse well in running water, remove skin, and pat dry.

2   Mince sardines well on a cutting board, transfer to a mortar, add cornstarch, salt, and soy sauce, and mash well with a pestle. When the mixture thickens, add egg, and mix well. Add ginger and scallions, mix well. (Food processor can also be used.)

3   Preheat oil to 340–350°F. Scoop sardine mixture with a teaspoon, forming balls, and deep-fry until golden brown and crispy outside. →❶

4   Serve sardine balls in small bowls, mound grated *daikon* on top, and add soy sauce.

◆ INGREDIENTS (4 servings)

21 oz sardines
2 Tbsp cornstarch
1/2 tsp salt
I tsp soy sauce
I egg
I Tbsp finely chopped fresh ginger
I Tbsp finely chopped scallions
6 Tbsp grated *daikon* radish
soy sauce
oil for deep-frying

茶わん蒸し

1人分 110 kcal

◆材　料 (4人分)

えび (30 gの殻つき、無頭)
　4尾
鶏もも肉 (皮なし)　80 g
生しいたけ　4枚
三つ葉　¼束 (15 g)
卵生地
　卵　3個
　だし　400 cc
　みりん　小さじ1
　薄口しょうゆ　小さじ2
　塩　少々
ゆずの皮 (細切り)　少々

◆作り方

1　えびは殻、背わたを取り、2～3等分に、
鶏肉は2cm角に切り、どちらも熱湯に
さっと通して、水でさまし、水けをきる。

2　しいたけは四つ割りにして、熱湯で
ゆでる。三つ葉は2cm長さに切る。

3　卵生地を作る。卵は泡立てないように
溶きほぐす。だしと調味料を混ぜ、
卵に加えて混ぜ合わせ、裏ごしする。→❶

4　1と2の汁けをきって、¼量ずつ器に入
れ、卵生地を8分目まで流し込む。
ふた (ラップでも可) をする。

5　蒸気の上がった蒸し器に入れ、
強火で2～3分、弱火で約15分蒸す。
竹串で刺してみて、澄んだ汁が出てきたら
蒸し上がり。→❷

6　蒸し器から取り出し、ゆずの皮を
のせる。

❶

❷

Savory Custard Cup

Chawan-mushi

110 kcal per serving

◆ DIRECTIONS

1 Shell and devein the shrimp, and cut each into 2–3 pieces. Cut chicken into ¾-inch cubes. Parboil shrimp and chicken briefly, cool in cold water, and drain.

2 Cut *shiitake* into quarters, and parboil. Cut *mitsuba* into ¾-inch lengths.

3 To make custard, beat eggs lightly so they won't bubble. Combine *dashi* and seasonings, add the mixture to the eggs, and strain through a sieve. →❶

4 Pat dry shrimp, chicken, *shiitake*, and *mitsuba*, and distribute evenly into 4 serving cups. Fill with custard to four-fifths full, and cover with lids or plastic wrap.

5 Transfer the cups to preheated steamer, and cook over high heat for 2–3 minutes. Turn down heat to low, and cook for 15 minutes more. Custard is done if clear juice comes out when it is poked with a bamboo skewer. →❷

6 Remove cups from steamer, open, and garnish with *yuzu* citron rind.

◆ INGREDIENTS (4 servings)

4 shrimp in shells without heads, 1 oz each
2 ⅘ oz chicken thighs, skinned
4 fresh *shiitake* mushrooms
¼ bunch (½ oz) *mitsuba* (trefoil)
Custard
[3 eggs
1⅔ U.S. cups *dashi*
1 tsp *mirin*
2 tsp light soy sauce
pinch salt
yuzu citron rind, thinly sliced

うなぎのかぶら蒸し

1人分 180 kcal

◆材 料(4人分)

うなぎ (かば焼き)
　½尾 (100 g)
えび (30 gの無頭)　4尾
しめじ　50 g
ぎんなん (水煮)　8個
三つ葉　¼束 (15 g)
かぶら生地
　[かぶら　1個 (300 g)
　　卵白　1個分
　　塩　少々]
べっこうあん
　[だし　300 cc
　　みりん　大さじ1
　　砂糖　大さじ1
　　しょうゆ　大さじ2
　　水溶き片栗粉
　　　[片栗粉　大さじ3
　　　　水　大さじ3]]
おろしわさび (→116頁)
　大さじ1

◆作り方

1　うなぎは2cm角に切る。えびは背わた、殻を取り、4等分にして、熱湯にさっと通す。しめじは石づきを切って小分けにし、熱湯でゆで、水けをきる。ぎんなんは縦半分に切り、三つ葉は軸だけにして3cm長さに切る。

2　かぶら生地を作る。卵白はよく溶く。かぶらの皮をむき、すりおろして、軽く水けを絞る。ボールにかぶら、卵白、塩少々を入れてよく混ぜる。

3　かぶら生地に具を混ぜ合わせ、1人用の器に、¼量をこんもりと盛る。

4　蒸気の上がった蒸し器に入れ、中火で約10分蒸す。

5　べっこうあんを作る。鍋にだし、調味料を煮立て、水溶き片栗粉を加え、とろみをつける。

6　かぶら蒸しに、熱々のあんをかけ、わさびをのせる。

Steamed Turnip and Eel in Amber Sauce

Unagi no Kabura-mushi

180 kcal per serving

◆ DIRECTIONS

1 Cut eel into ¾-inch squares. Shell and devein shrimp, cut each into 4 pieces, and briefly parboil. Separate *shimeji* into small clusters, parboil, and drain. Cut gingko nuts in half lengthwise. Discard leaves of *mitsuba*, and cut stems into 1-inch lengths.

2 To make turnip mixture: Beat egg white. Peel turnip, grate, and wring lightly. Combine turnip, egg white, and salt in a bowl, and mix well.

3 Add prepared ingredients to turnip mixture, and mix. Mound in individual serving bowls.

4 Transfer bowls to a preheated steamer and cook over medium heat for 10 minutes.

5 To make amber sauce: Heat *dashi* and seasonings in a saucepan, and bring to a boil. Add starch-water mixture to thicken.

6 Pour hot sauce into each bowl, and garnish with grated *wasabi*.

◆ INGREDIENTS (4 servings)

½ (3½ oz) grilled
  unagi eel
4 shrimp in shells without
  heads, 1 oz each
1¾ oz *shimeji* mushrooms
8 ginkgo nuts, boiled
¼ bunch (½ oz)
  mitsuba (trefoil)
Turnip Mixture
  ⎰ 1 (10½ oz) turnip
  ⎱ 1 egg white
  ⎰ pinch salt
Amber Sauce
  ⎰ 1¼ U.S. cups *dashi*
  ⎱ 1 Tbsp *mirin*
  ⎰ 1 Tbsp sugar
  ⎱ 2 Tbsp soy sauce
  ⎰ starch-water mixture
    ⎰ 3 Tbsp cornstarch
    ⎱ 3 Tbsp water
1 Tbsp grated *wasabi*
  horseradish (→p. 117)

あさりの酒蒸し

1人分 30 kcal

◆材　料(4人分)

あさり　20個 (400 g)
塩　適量
長ねぎ　5 cm
酒　200 cc
薄口しょうゆ　小さじ1

◆作り方

1　あさりは塩水（水200ccに塩小さじ1の割合）につけて砂を吐かせる。殻と殻をこすりつけて、よく洗う。→❶

2　長ねぎは縦に切り込みを入れ、芯を取って細いせん切りにする。→❷

3　鍋にあさりを入れ、酒を加え、ふたをして強火にかける。

4　殻が開いたら、薄口しょうゆで味を調える。

5　あさりを汁とともに器に盛り、長ねぎをのせる。

❶

❷

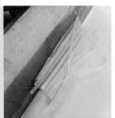

Saké-Steamed Clams

Asari no Saka-mushi

30 kcal per serving

◆ DIRECTIONS

1 Let the clams stand in salted water (1 tsp salt to 6²/₃ oz water) to allow them to expel sand. Wash clams well, rubbing shells against each other. →❶

2 Slit leek lengthwise, remove core, and slice into fine julienne strips. →❷

3 Place clams in a skillet, add *saké*, cover, and heat on high.

4 When clams are open, season with light soy sauce.

5 Serve clams with pan juices, and garnish with leek.

◆ INGREDIENTS (4 servings)

20 (14 oz) live littleneck clams

salt

2-inch Japanese leek

6²/₃ oz *saké*

1 tsp light soy sauce

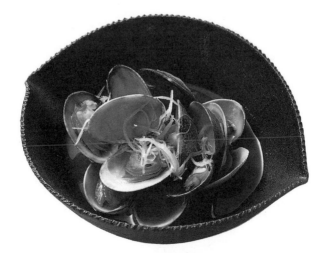

ざるそば

1人分 310 kcal

◆材 料(4人分)

生そば(または乾麺) 4玉
つけ汁
- だし 400 cc
- みりん 大さじ4
- 砂糖 大さじ2
- しょうゆ 大さじ6

薬味
- 焼きのり 1/2枚
- さらしねぎ(→32頁)
  大さじ4
- 大根おろし 大さじ4
- おろしわさび(→116頁)
  大さじ2

◆作り方

1 つけ汁を作る。鍋にみりんを入れて
一煮立ちさせ、だし、砂糖、しょうゆを
加えて再び煮立ったら火をとめ、さます。
器に移して冷蔵庫で冷やす。

2 たっぷりの湯を沸かし、煮立ったら
生そばを入れ、ゆでる。ゆで上がったら、
流水でよくもみ洗いし、ぬめりを取る。
ざるに上げて水けをきる。→❶❷

3 そばを盛り、細かくちぎった焼きのりを
散らし、つけ汁、薬味を添える。

Chilled *Soba* Noodles with *Nori*

Zaru Soba

310 kcal per serving

◆ DIRECTIONS

1 To make dipping sauce: Place *mirin* in a saucepan, and bring to a boil, add *dashi*, sugar, and soy sauce. When it boils for the second time, remove from heat, and let stand to cool. When cool, transfer to a bowl, and chill in the refrigerator.

2 Boil a generous amount of hot water, and cook fresh *soba* noodles. When done, rinse in cold running water, squeezing and turning the noodles with one hand to get rid of stickiness. Drain in a sieve. →❶❷

3 Arrange the noodles on serving plates with flaked *nori* pieces on top, and serve with dipping sauce, and other condiments.

◆ INGREDIENTS (4 servings)

4 portions fresh or dried *soba* noodles

Dipping Sauce
- 1²/₃ U.S. cups *dashi*
- 4 Tbsp *mirin*
- 2 Tbsp sugar
- 6 Tbsp soy sauce

Condiments
- ¹/₂ sheet *nori* seaweed, toasted
- 4 Tbsp rinsed scallions (→p. 33)
- 4 Tbsp grated *daikon* radish
- 2 Tbsp grated *wasabi* horseradish (→p. 117)

❶

❷

鴨南蛮そば

1人分 390 kcal

◆材　料(4人分)

生そば　4玉
合鴨胸肉*　1枚 (400 g)
青ねぎ　8本
そばつゆ
 ┌ だし　1600 cc
 │ 砂糖　小さじ2
 │ 塩　小さじ⅓
 └ しょうゆ　大さじ6
粉ざんしょう　少々

*鴨肉の代わりに鶏肉を使
えば、鶏南蛮になる。

◆作り方

1　鴨肉は筋や余分な脂を切り取り、
薄くそぎ切りにする。青ねぎは、
斜め薄切りにする。

2　たっぷりの湯を沸かし、煮立ったら
生そばを入れ、ゆでる。ゆで上がったら、
流水でよくもみ洗いし、ざるに上げて
水けをきる。

3　鍋にそばつゆの材料を入れて
煮立たせ、鴨肉、青ねぎを加えて
軽く煮る。

4　食べる直前に、そばを沸騰している
湯に通して温め、水けをきる。

5　器に盛り、鴨肉、青ねぎをのせて、
煮汁をかけ、好みで粉ざんしょうをふる。

Duck *Nanban Soba* Noodles

Kamo-nanban Soba

390 kcal per serving

◆ DIRECTIONS

1 Trim any tendons and excess fat from duck breast, and slice thinly. Cut scallions diagonally into thin slices.

2 Boil a generous amount of water, and cook fresh *soba* noodles. When done, rinse with cold running water, squeezing and turning the noodles with one hand to get rid of stickiness. Drain in a sieve.

3 Combine broth ingredients in a pot, bring to a boil, add duck and scallions, and cook briefly.

4 Just before serving, reheat *soba* noodles quickly by dipping in boiling water, and drain.

5 Transfer into bowls, add duck meat and scallions, pour broth over, and sprinkle with ground *sansho* pepper to taste.

◆ INGREDIENTS (4 servings)

4 portions fresh *soba* noodles

1 (14 oz) duck breast *

8 scallions

Broth
- 6 1/2 u.s. cups *dashi*
- 2 tsp sugar
- 1/3 tsp salt
- 6 Tbsp soy sauce

ground *sansho* pepper

* Chicken can be substituted for duck to make "chicken *Nanban soba* noodles."

鍋焼きうどん

1人分 400 kcal

◆材　料(4人分)

ゆでうどん　4玉
えびのてんぷら (→186頁)
　4尾
かまぼこ　50 g
しいたけの甘煮 (→82頁)
　4枚
卵　4個
春菊　½束 (100 g)
うどんつゆ
　だし　1500 cc
　薄口しょうゆ　大さじ6
　砂糖　小さじ2
　みりん　大さじ2
　塩　小さじ⅔
七味唐がらし　少々

◆作り方

1　具を用意し、かまぼこ、しいたけの甘煮は薄切りにする。

2　鍋にうどんつゆを合わせ、一煮立ちさせる。

3　ゆでうどんはさっと水で洗い、水けをきる。

4　1人用の土鍋にうどんを入れ、えびのてんぷら、かまぼこ、しいたけを盛り、うどんつゆを注ぐ。

5　中火で約5分煮て、卵を真ん中に割り入れ、春菊を加えて火をとめ、ふたをして蒸らす。好みで七味唐がらしをふる。

Udon Noodles in Clay Pots

Nabe-yaki Udon

400 kcal per serving

◆ DIRECTIONS

1 Prepare tempura, and simmered *shiitake*. Cut kamaboko fishcake and simmered *shiitake* into thin slices.

2 Combine broth ingredients in a pot, and bring to a boil.

3 Rinse *udon* noodles lightly in cold water, and drain.

4 Place noodles in individual clay pots, distribute shrimp tempura, *kamaboko* fishcake, and simmered *shiitake* evenly, and pour broth over.

5 Cook over medium heat about 5 minutes, crack an egg into the middle of each pot, add chrysanthemum leaves, remove from heat, and cover to steam for a while. Sprinkle with seven-spice pepper to taste.

◆ INGREDIENTS (4 servings)

4 portions boiled *udon* noodles

4 shrimp tempura (→p. 187)

1 3/4 oz *kamaboko* fishcake

4 simmered *shiitake* mushrooms (→p. 83)

4 eggs

1/2 bunch (3 1/2 oz) chrysanthemum leaves

Broth
- 6 1/4 U.S. cups *dashi*
- 6 Tbsp light soy sauce
- 2 tsp sugar
- 2 Tbsp *mirin*
- 2/3 tsp salt

seven-spice pepper

カレーうどん

1人分 460 kcal

◆材　料 (4人分)

ゆでうどん　4玉
牛ロース肉 (薄切り)　200 g
玉ねぎ　½個 (70 g)
青ねぎ　1束
カレー汁
　だし　1700 cc
　砂糖　大さじ2
　塩　小さじ1
　こしょう　少々
　しょうゆ　大さじ3
　カレールウ　70 g
　水溶き片栗粉
　　片栗粉　大さじ3〜4
　　水　大さじ3〜4
サラダ油　適量

◆作り方

1　牛肉は一口大に切る。玉ねぎは薄切り、青ねぎは斜め薄切りにする。

2　鍋に油を熱し、肉、玉ねぎをいため、しんなりとしてきたら、だし、砂糖、塩、こしょう、しょうゆを入れて煮る。

3　カレールウを加え、さらに3分ほど煮、水溶き片栗粉でとろみをつける。火をとめる直前に青ねぎを加える。

4　沸騰している湯でうどんを温め、水けをよくきる。

5　器に盛り、熱々のカレー汁をたっぷりかける。

Udon Noodles with Curry Sauce

Karē Udon

460 kcal per serving

◆ DIRECTIONS

1   Cut beef into bite-sized pieces. Slice onion thinly, chop scallions diagonally into thin slices.

2   Heat oil in a skillet, and sauté beef and onion until tender. Add *dashi*, sugar, salt, pepper, and soy sauce, and simmer.

3   Add curry roux, cook 3 more minutes, and add starch-water mixture to thicken. Add scallions just before removing from heat.

4   Heat *udon* noodles in boiling water, and drain.

5   Transfer noodles to bowls, and top with generous amount of hot curry sauce.

◆ INGREDIENTS (4 servings)

4 portions boiled *udon* noodles

7 oz beef loin, thinly sliced

$1/2$ ($2 1/2$ oz) onion

1 bunch scallions

Curry Sauce

  $7 1/5$ U.S. cups *dashi*

  2 Tbsp sugar

  1 tsp salt

  pinch pepper

  3 Tbsp soy sauce

  $2 1/2$ oz curry roux

  starch-water mixture

    3–4 Tbsp cornstarch

    3–4 Tbsp water

vegetable oil

釜上げうどん

1人分 220 kcal

◆材　料(4人分)

生うどん　600 g

つけ汁
- だし　400 cc
- みりん　大さじ2
- 砂糖　小さじ1
- 薄口しょうゆ　大さじ2
- しょうゆ　大さじ4

薬味
- さらしねぎ(→32頁)
  　大さじ4
- おろししょうが　大さじ2
- 白いりごま　大さじ2

◆作り方

1　つけ汁の材料を鍋に入れて一煮立ちさせ、器に入れる。

2　たっぷりの湯を沸かし、うどんをゆでる。途中2～3回差し水をする(めんによってゆでる時間が違う)。ゆで汁ごと食卓に出せる器に移す。

3　好みの薬味を入れ、つけ汁につけて食べる。

Udon Noodles in a Pot

Kama-age Udon

220 kcal per serving

◆ DIRECTIONS

1 Combine dipping sauce ingredients in a saucepan, and bring to a boil.

2 Boil a generous amount of hot water, and cook *udon* noodles. Add a little cold water 2–3 times during cooking. (Cooking time differs according to noodle type: Follow noodle package instructions). Transfer noodles and hot water used for boiling into serving bowls.

3 Add condiments to dipping sauce, and dip noodles before eating, bite by bite.

◆ INGREDIENTS (4 servings)

21 oz fresh *udon* noodles

Dipping Sauce

- 1²/₃ U.S. cups *dashi*
- 2 Tbsp *mirin*
- 1 tsp sugar
- 2 Tbsp light soy sauce
- 4 Tbsp soy sauce

Condiments

- 4 Tbsp rinsed scallions (→p. 33)
- 2 Tbsp grated fresh ginger
- 2 Tbsp white sesame seeds, toasted

冷やしそうめん

1人分 460 kcal

◆材 料(4人分)

そうめん 4束(300g)
つけ汁
    だし 500cc
    みりん 大さじ5
    薄口しょうゆ 大さじ5
    干しえび 30g
えび(30gの無頭) 4尾
薄焼き卵(→82頁) 2枚
しいたけの甘煮(→82頁)
    4枚
三つ葉 1束(50g)
薬味
    おろししょうが 大さじ2
    さらしねぎ(→32頁)
    大さじ4
塩 適量

◆作り方

1 つけ汁を作る。鍋にみりんを一煮立ちさせ、だし、薄口しょうゆ、干しえびを加え、再び煮立ったら火をとめ、さます。器に移して冷蔵庫で冷やす。

2 えびは背わたを取り、串をうち、塩ゆでにする。さめたら殻をむき、腹開きにする。

3 薄焼き卵、しいたけは細切りにする。

4 三つ葉はさっと塩ゆでにし、2cm長さに切る。

5 たっぷりの沸騰した湯にそうめんを入れ、すぐに箸でかき混ぜてめんを沈める。ふきこぼれそうになったら、差し水をする。再び煮立ってきたら火をとめ、ざるに上げ、流水でよくもみ洗いし、水けをきる。→❶❷❸

6 器にそうめんを盛り、えび、しいたけ、薄焼き卵、三つ葉を添える。

7 つけ汁につけ、好みの薬味を入れて食べる。

❶

❷

❸

Chilled *Somen* Noodles

Hiyashi Sōmen

460 kcal per serving

◆ DIRECTIONS

1 To make dipping sauce: Bring *mirin* to a boil, and add *dashi*, light soy sauce, dried shrimp. When it boils for the second time, remove from heat and cool. Transfer to a bowl and chill in the refrigerator.

2 Devein and skewer shrimp, and parboil in lightly salted water. When cool, shell, and slit open from underside.

3 Cut thin omelette and *shiitake* mushrooms into thin strips.

4 Parboil *mitsuba* briefly in lightly salted water, and cut into ¾-inch lengths.

5 Place *somen* noodles in ample boiling water, and stir with chopsticks to make the noodles sink. When about to boil over, add a small amount of cold water. When it boils for the second time, remove from heat, drain, and rinse in cold running water, squeezing and turning the noodles with one hand. Drain.→❶❷❸

6 Transfer to serving plates, and arrange shrimp, *shiitake*, thin omelette, and *mitsuba* on top.

7 When eating, add condiments to the dipping sauce to taste, and dip noodles as you go.

◆ INGREDIENTS (4 servings)

4 bundles (10½ oz) *somen* noodles

Dipping Sauce

- 2⅛ U.S. cups *dashi*
- 5 Tbsp *mirin*
- 5 Tbsp light soy sauce
- 1 oz dried shrimp

4 shrimp in shells without heads, 1 oz each

2 thin omelettes (→p. 83)

4 simmered *shiitake* mushrooms (→p. 83)

1 bunch (1¾ oz) *mitsuba* (trefoil)

2 Tbsp grated fresh ginger

4 Tbsp rinsed scallions (→p. 33)

salt

あずきあん

100 g 320 kcal

◆材料 (約450gのつぶしあん)

あずき　150 g
砂糖　230 g
水飴　10 g
塩　少々

◆作り方

1　あずきはよく洗って鍋に入れ、たっぷりの水に4〜5時間つける。そのまま火にかけ、沸騰したら差し水(200cc)をし、再び沸騰してきたら、ざるに上げ、水けをきる。

2　新しい水を鍋に入れ、あずきが柔らかくなるまでゆでる。ゆで汁は常に豆がかぶるくらい補うこと。再びざるに上げ、水けをきる。

3　あずきを鍋に戻して分量の砂糖を加え、よく混ぜ合わせ、火にかけ、静かに混ぜながら煮つめる。

4　水飴を加えて煮溶かす。→❶

5　仕上げに塩を加え、さっと混ぜて火をとめる。

❶

Sweet Red-Bean Paste

Azuki-an

320 kcal per 3¹/₂ oz

◆ DIRECTIONS

1 In a pot, soak well-rinsed *azuki* beans in ample water for 4–5 hours. Heat until boiling, then add 6²/₃ oz of water. When it boils for the second time, drain in a sieve.

2 In fresh water, boil beans again until tender. Add water so the liquid always covers beans while cooking. Drain again in a sieve.

3 Transfer beans back to pot, add sugar, and mix well. Cook down over low heat, stirring gently.

4 Add *mizuame* syrup, heating until melted. →❶

5 Add pinch salt to finish, stir lightly, and remove from heat.

◆ INGREDIENTS
(Makes 16 oz paste)

5¹/₄ oz *azuki* red beans
8 oz sugar
¹/₃ oz *mizuame* syrup
  (or honey)
pinch salt

ぜんざい

1人分 470 kcal

◆材　料(4人分)

もち　4個
あずきあん (→224頁)
　　400 g
水　800 cc
砂糖　30 g
塩　小さじ½
塩昆布 (あれば)　適量

◆作り方

1　もちは一口大に切り、焼き網で
あまり焦がさないように柔らかく焼く。→❶

2　鍋にあずきあん、水、砂糖、塩を
入れて少し煮つめる。

3　器に焼いたもちを入れ、熱々のあんを
注ぐ。塩昆布を小皿に入れて添える。

❶

Sweet Red-Bean Soup with Rice Cakes

Zenzai

470 kcal per serving

◆ DIRECTIONS

1   Cut rice cakes into bite-sized pieces, and broil on a cooking grill until tender. Do not brown. →❶

2   Place red-bean paste, water, sugar, and salt in a soup pot, and cook down briefly.

3   Transfer rice cakes to serving bowls, and pour hot bean soup over. Serve with salted *konbu* kelp in a small dish on the side.

◆ INGREDIENTS (4 servings)

4 rice cakes

14 oz sweet red-bean paste (→p. 225)

3 1/3 U.S. cups water

1 oz sugar

1/2 tsp salt

salted *konbu* kelp as condiment

どら焼き

1個分 190 kcal

◆材　料（直径10cm8個分）

生地
- 卵　3個 (160 g)
- 砂糖　150 g
- 重曹　小さじ½
- 水　約50 cc
- 小麦粉　200 g

あずきあん (→224頁)
　400 g

サラダ油　適量

◆作り方

1　ボールに卵を割り、泡立て器で溶きほぐし、砂糖を加えてよく混ぜ合わせる。白っぽく、ドロッとした状態になるまで泡立てる。

2　重曹を小さじ1の水で溶いて加え、分量の水½量を加えてよく混ぜる。

3　ふるった小麦粉を加えて混ぜ合わせ、残りの水を少しずつ入れて、生地をゆるめる。

4　平たい鉄板に油少量を熱し、玉じゃくし約1杯分の生地を落とし、きれいな円形に焼く。→❶

5　上面が半乾きになり泡が浮いてプップツと穴があいてきたら、下側をのぞいて、きれいなキツネ色になっていたらひっくり返し、裏は乾かす程度に焼く。→❷

6　焼きあがった皮がさめたら2枚1組にし、あんを約25gはさんで軽く押さえ、形を整える。

❶

❷

Sweet Bean "Gongs"

Dora-yaki

190 kcal per "gong"

◆ DIRECTIONS

1   Beat eggs in a bowl with a whisk, add sugar, and mix well. Beat the egg mixture until whitish and stringy.

2   Mix baking soda with 1 tsp water, and add to the egg mixture. Add half of the measured water, and mix well.

3   Stir in sifted flour, then add rest of the water gradually into batter, mixing.

4   Heat a lightly oiled griddle, and pour 1 ladle of batter on, making a round shape, and cook. →❶

5   When top surface is half dry and bubbles, check if the bottom is golden brown, and turn over to cook until dry. →❷

6   Sort cooled pancakes into pairs. Spread ⅞ oz red-bean paste on a pancake, cover with another, and press lightly to secure.

◆ INGREDIENTS (Makes 8 [4-inch] filled "gongs")

Pancakes

3 (5⅖ oz) eggs
5¼ oz sugar
½ tsp baking soda
about 1⅔ oz water
7 oz flour

14 oz red-bean paste
  (→p. 225)
vegetable oil

みたらしだんご

1本分 110 kcal

◆材　料 (12本分)

白玉粉　200 g
ぬるま湯　約190 cc
たれ
 水　300 cc
 昆布　10 g
 砂糖　120 g
 水飴　30 g
 しょうゆ　大さじ2
 水溶き片栗粉
  片栗粉　大さじ1½
  水　大さじ1½

◆作り方

1　ボールに白玉粉を入れ、ぬるま湯を少しずつ加え、手でよく練り、耳たぶのかたさにする。

2　小さく丸めて (約30g)、沸騰した湯の中に入れ約5分ゆでる。4個ずつ串に刺す。

3　たれを作る。鍋に分量の水と昆布を入れ、火にかけ、沸騰直前に昆布を取り出し、砂糖、水飴、しょうゆを入れて弱火にし、煮立ってきたら、水溶き片栗粉を加え、とろみをつける。

4　だんごを刺した串を焼き網の上でうっすらと焦げ目がつく程度に焼く。

5　だんごにたれをたっぷりからめる。

Skewered Dumplings with Brown Sauce

Mitarashi Dango

110kcal per skewer

◆ DIRECTIONS

1 Place rice flour in a bowl and add lukewarm water gradually, kneading, until dough becomes "as hard as your earlobes."

2 Make small dumplings (1 oz each) with the dough, boil in hot water for 5 minutes, and skewer 4 to each stick.

3 To make sauce: Place water and *konbu* in a soup pot over medium heat. Remove *konbu* just before water reaches a boil. Add sugar, *mizuame* syrup, and soy sauce, turn down the heat to low. When it boils, add starch-water mixture to thicken.

4 Grill skewered dumplings on a cooking grill until light brown.

5 Brush brown sauce generously on dumplings.

◆ INGREDIENTS
  (Makes 12 skewers)

7 oz glutinous rice flour
about 3/4 U.S. cup
  lukewarm water
Sauce
⎧ 1 1/4 U.S. cups water
⎪ 1/3 oz *konbu* kelp
⎪ 4 1/5 oz sugar
⎨ 1 oz *mizuame* syrup
⎪   (or honey)
⎪ 2 Tbsp soy sauce
⎩ starch-water mixture
    ⎧ 1 1/2 Tbsp cornstarch
    ⎩ 1 1/2 Tbsp water

豆かん

1人分 150 kcal

◆材　料(4人分)

赤えんどう豆　30 g
重曹　小さじ½
寒天生地
- 寒天　⅓本
- 水　200 cc
- 砂糖　大さじ1
黒みつ
- 黒砂糖　50 g
- 砂糖　50 g
- 水飴　大さじ1
- 水　100 cc

◆作り方

1　赤えんどう豆は熱湯に重曹を入れた中でゆで、一煮立ちしたら火をとめ、そのまま1晩つける。えんどう豆の水けをきり、蒸気の上がった蒸し器に入れ、柔らかく蒸し、さます。

2　寒天は水に浸し、落としぶたをして2時間つけてもどす。手で小さくちぎり、水けを絞って、分量の水に入れ、初め強火、煮立ったら弱火にして煮溶かし、完全に溶けたら、砂糖を加える。

3　水でぬらした型に流し入れ、冷やし固める。完全に固まったら1cm角に切る。

4　黒みつを作る。鍋に黒砂糖、砂糖、水飴(はちみつでも可)、水を一煮立ちさせ、1割煮つめたら、さます。器に移して冷蔵庫で冷やす。

5　よく冷やした器に盛りつけ、黒みつをかける。

Japanese Jello
Mamekan

150 kcal per serving

◆ DIRECTIONS

1 Add *endo* peas to boiling water with baking soda. When water boils up again, remove from heat, and let stand overnight. Drain, steam until tender in a piping-hot steamer, and cool.

2 To make agar-agar jelly: Soak agar-agar stick in water with a drop-lid; let stand for 2 hours. Tear softened agar-agar stick into pieces, wring out moisture, and place in a saucepan with the measured water. Heat over high until boiling, and turn down to low. When melted completely, add sugar.

3 Pour into a wet square baking pan, and cool until fully thickened. Cut jelly into ³⁄₈-inch cubes.

4 To make dark syrup: Combine all ingredients in a saucepan, and boil off 10% of original amount. Cool, transfer to a bowl, and let chilled in a refrigerator.

5 Arrange agar-agar cubes and peas in chilled serving bowls, and pour dark syrup over.

◆ INGREDIENTS (4 servings)

1³⁄₄ oz *endo* (red monkey) peas
¹⁄₂ tsp baking soda
Agar-Agar Jelly
  ⌈ ¹⁄₃ stick agar-agar
  │ 6²⁄₃ oz water
  ⌊ 1 Tbsp sugar
Dark Syrup
  ⌈ 1³⁄₄ oz brown sugar
  │ 1³⁄₄ oz sugar
  ⟨ 1 Tbsp *mizuame* syrup
  │   (or honey)
  ⌊ 3¹⁄₃ oz water

大学芋

1人分 280 kcal

◆材 料(4人分)

さつま芋 400 g
砂糖 80 g
水 大さじ2
しょうゆ 小さじ2
黒ごま 小さじ1
揚げ油 適量

◆作り方

1 さつま芋は皮をむいて一口大の
乱切りにし、水にさらす。→❶

2 水けをふき取り、170℃の揚げ油で
カリッとキツネ色に揚げる。→❷

3 鍋に砂糖、水、しょうゆを入れて煮立て、
つやが出て糸を引くようになったら、
揚げたてのさつま芋とごまを加えて
からめる。

❶

❷

Candied Sweet Potatoes
Daigaku-imo

280 kcal per serving

◆ DIRECTIONS

1 Peel sweet potatoes, and cut roughly into bite-sized pieces, and soak in water. →❶

2 Pat dry, and deep-fry at 340°F until crispy and golden brown. →❷

3 Place sugar, water, and soy sauce in a pan, and bring to a boil. When glossy and sticky, add deep-fried potatoes and sesame seeds, and mix to coat.

◆ INGREDIENTS (4 servings)

14 oz sweet potatoes
2 ⁴/₅ oz sugar
2 Tbsp water
2 tsp soy sauce
1 tsp black sesame seeds
oil for deep-frying

献立の立て方

● 献立の基本

　日本料理の献立では、一汁三菜が基本となります。一汁つまり汁物が一品と、生もの、焼き物、煮物を合わせた三菜です。焼き物、煮物のかわりに蒸し物、揚げ物を持ってきたり、あるいは基本の三菜にそれらをプラスしたり、さらに酢の物、あえ物を添えたりと変化させていきます。

● 季節感を織り込む

　四季おりおりの産物が豊かな風土で生まれ育った日本料理では、季節感をたいせつにしています。献立全体に季節を表現して、旬の材料をたっぷり盛り込んだ料理や演出でいただきたいと思います。

● バランスよく組み合わせる

　もてなしに有利なのは、得意の料理を持つこと。自慢できる料理があれば、それを中心にして、起承転結を考えながら残りの料理を選べば自然に献立ができあがるはずです。この場合、五味の配分、味の濃淡の変化、冷温のバラエティーなど欠くことのできない条件になります。献立の中に、あたたかいもの、冷たいものがバランスよく配置されているか、同じ材料が何ヵ所にも重なったり、濃い味のものが続いたり、また逆に薄味のものばかりになったりしていないかチェックしてみます。

　また、品数が少なめのときには、ごはんを変わりごはんやおすしにして、たっぷり召し上がっていただくような工夫も必要です。

● 食器と盛りつけ

　日本料理は目でも楽しむものですから、食器の選び方や盛りつけにも心を配りたいものです。料理に合わせて形、色、材質に変化をつけたり、季節感をいっそう高めることを心がけてください。

MENU PLANNING

● The Basic Menu

The phrase *ichiju sansai*, "Soup plus Three," describes the basic structure of a Japanese meal. In other words, a Japanese menu typically consists of soup and three entrees: a dish of fresh, uncooked fish, a grilled dish, and a simmered dish. Steamed or deep-fried dishes may be served in place of the grilled or simmered ones, or you can simply add them on to the basic menu of "Soup plus Three." Vinegared dishes or dressed salads can also be included as variations.

● A Sense for the Season

Because Japanese cuisine developed in close relation to nature's seasonally changing bounty, a sense for the season plays an important role in any Japanese meal. Mirror the time of year throughout the menu by generously including seasonal ingredients.

● Harmony

Having a specialty is a big help when organizing a dinner party. Plan the menu around a special dish, keeping in mind that the meal should flow smoothly from beginning to middle to end. Take care to distribute the five flavors evenly and to vary the seasoning and food temperature. The number of hot and cold foods should be balanced. Avoid using the same ingredients in different dishes. Don't serve only strongly seasoned dishes or only lightly seasoned ones. If the menu contains only a small number or entrees, augment it by serving in place of plain rice several different prepared rice dishes or sushi.

● Tableware and Arrangement

Japanese cuisine should delight the eye as well as the taste buds. Take special care in selecting tableware and arranging the food. Try to vary the shapes, colors, and materials of your tableware according to what you serve, and try to bring forth a seasonal sense.

四季の献立例 • MENUS FOR THE FOUR SEASONS

春 SPRING

はまぐりのうしお汁　Clam Soup　*38•39*
そぼろ丼　Minced Chicken and Egg Bowl　*66•67*
豆腐田楽　Tofu *Dengaku*　*154•155*
めばるの煮つけ　Simmered Rockfish　*174•175*
焼きしいたけポン酢あえ
　　Grilled Mushrooms with Lemon-Soy Sauce　*96•97*

かきたま汁　Beaten Egg Soup　*34•35*
豆ご飯　Green Pea Rice　*54•55*
たいの薄造り中華風ドレッシング
　　Sea Bream Sashimi with Chinese Dressing　*118•119*
牛肉の照り焼き　Steak Teriyaki　*148•149*
高野豆腐の含め煮　Simmered Freeze-Dried Tofu　*168•169*
みたらしだんご　Skewered Dumplings with Brown Sauce　*230•231*

夏 SUMMER

貝柱の沢煮わん　Scallop and Vegetable Soup, *Sawa*-style　*40•41*
ばらずし　Scattered Sushi　*82•83*
焼きなす　Grilled Eggplant　*138•139*
きんぴらごぼう　Sautéed Burdock, *Kimpira*-style　*160•161*
鶏南蛮漬け　Chicken Escabeche, *Nanban*-style　*102•103*

豆腐とわかめのみそ汁
　　Tofu and *Wakame* Seaweed Miso Soup　*32•33*
天丼　Tempura Bow　*62•63*
クレソンのお浸し　Marinated Watercress　*92•93*
だし巻き卵　Rolled Omelette　*140•141*
ひじきのいため煮　Braised *Hijiki* Seaweed　*166•167*
豆かん　Japanese Jello　*232•233*

秋 AUTUMN

えびだんごのすまし汁　Clear Soup with Shrimp Balls　*42•43*

栗ご飯　Chestnut Rice　*52•53*

オクラと長芋のわさびじょうゆあえ
　Okra and Mountain Yams with *Wasabi* Sauce　*104•105*

さばのみそ煮　Simmered Mackerel in Miso　*176•177*

てんぷら　Tempura　*186•187*

どら焼き　Sweet Bean "Gongs"　*228•229*

豚汁　Miso Soup with Pork and Vegetables　*36•37*

さけの混ぜご飯　Salmon and Pickle Rice　*68•69*

鶏の竜田揚げ　Deep-Fried Marinated Chicken　*190•191*

かに酢　Vinegared Crab and Cucumber　*94•95*

白菜と薄揚げの旨煮
　Simmered Chinese Cabbage with Deep-Fried Tofu　*164•165*

冬 WINTER

茶わん蒸し　Savory Custard Cup　*206•207*

赤飯　Red Rice with *Azuki* Beans　*56•57*

まぐろのおろし造り　Tuna Sashimi with Grated Radish　*116•117*

肉じゃが　Braised Meat and Potatoes　*158•159*

焼きはまぐり　Salt-Grilled Clams　*142•143*

ぜんざい　Sweet Red-Bean Soup with Rice Cakes　*226•227*

けんちん汁　Tofu, Pork, and Vegetable Soup, *Kenchin*-style　*44•45*

ご飯　Boiled Rice　*48•49*

おでん　*Oden* Stew　*130•131*

ほうれん草のごまあえ　Spinach with Sesame Dressing　*90•91*

牛肉サラダ　Beef Salad　*100•101*

度量衡早見表 • MEASUREMENTS

容量／LIQUID MEASURE

小さじ1 = 1 tsp = 5 ml (cc)
大さじ1 = 1 Tbsp = 15 ml (cc)
1 Japanese cup = 200 ml
1 American (U.S.) cup = 240 (236) ml

SPOONS	MILLILITERS	U.S. CUPS	OUNCES
1 tsp	5 ml		
1 Tbsp	15 ml		
3 Tbsp+1 tsp	47 ml (50 ml)	1/5 cup	1 2/3 oz
4 Tbsp	59 ml	1/4 cup	
5 Tbsp+1 tsp	79 ml	1/3 cup	
7 Tbsp−1 tsp	94 ml (100 ml)	2/5 cup	3 1/3 oz
8 Tbsp	118 ml (120 ml)	1/2 cup	
10 Tbsp	142 ml (150 ml)	3/5 cup	5 oz
13 Tbsp+1 tsp	200 ml	4/5 cup	6 2/3 oz
16 Tbsp	236 ml (240 ml)	1 cup	8 oz
	296 ml (300 ml)	1 1/4 cups	10 oz
	394 ml (400 ml)	1 2/3 cups	
	473 ml	2 cups	
	500 ml	2 1/8 cups	
	560 ml	2 2/5 cups	19 oz
	600 ml	2 1/2 cups	
	710 ml	3 cups	
	800 ml	3 1/3 cups	
	946 ml (1 liter)	4 cups	

長さ／LINEAR MEASURE

inches × 2.54 = centimeters
centimeters × .39 = inches

CENTIMETERS	INCHES
1 1/2 mm	1/16 in
3 mm	1/8 in
5 mm	3/16 in
1 cm	3/8 in
1 1/2 cm	1/2 in (5/8 in)
2 cm	3/4 in
2 1/2 cm	1 in
4 cm	1 1/2 in
5 cm	2 in
6 1/2 cm	2 1/2 in
8 cm	3 in
9 cm	3 1/2 in
10 cm	4 in

重量／WEIGHTS

grams × 0.035 = ounces

ounces × 28.35 = grams

GRAMS	OUNCES	POUNDS
5 g	1/6 oz	
10 g	1/3 oz	
15 g	1/2 oz	
20 g	2/3 oz	
30 g	1 oz	
50 g	1¾ oz	
60 g	2 oz	
70 g	2½ oz	
80 g	2⅘ oz	
85 g	3 oz	
100 g	3½ oz	
115 g	4 oz	¼ lb
140 g	5 oz	
150 g	5¼ oz	
170 g	6 oz	
200 g	7 oz	
225 g	8 oz	½ lb
300 g	10½ oz	
340 g	12 oz	¾ lb
360 g	12⅔ oz	
400 g	14 oz	
450 g	16 oz	1 lb
500 g	18 oz	
600 g	21 oz	
700 g	24½ oz	
800 g	28 oz	1¾ lb

温度／TEMPERATURE

$$Fahrenheit = \frac{Centigrade \times 9}{5} + 32$$

$$Centigrade = \frac{(Fahrenheit - 32) \times 5}{9}$$

DEEP-FRYING OIL TEMPERATURES
160°C / 320°F – 165°C / 330°F = low
170°C / 340°F – 175°C / 350°F = medium
175°C / 350°F – 180°C / 360°F = high

基本的な切り方 • BASIC CUTTING TECHNIQUES

輪切り
wa-giri
rounds

大根や人参など円筒形の材料を小口から横に一定の厚さで切る。

Slice cylindrical foods like *daikon* radishes and carrots crosswise into rounds of uniform thickness.

くし形切り
kushigata-giri
wedge cut

レモンなど球形の材料を縦の放射状に4〜6等分に切る。

Cut spherical foods like lemons lengthwise into four to six wedges.

半月切り
hangetsu-giri
half-moons

円筒形を縦半分にしてから、小口から横に一定の厚さで切る。

Cut a cylinder in half lengthwise, then slice crosswise into half-moons of uniform thickness.

短冊切り
tanzaku-giri
rectangles

細長い角形のものを繊維に添って長方形の薄切り。

Cut a rectangular block into thin slabs with the grain running in the same direction as the cut.

いちょう切り
ichō-giri
quarter-rounds

円筒形を縦1/4にして小口から横に一定の厚さで切る。

Cut a cylinder in quarters lengthwise, then slice crosswise into quarter-rounds of uniform thickness.

拍子木切り
hyōshigi-giri
bar rectangles

細長い角形のものを1cm角、4cm長さの棒状に切る。

Cut a rectangular block into 3/8 × 3/8 × 1½-inch bars.

せん切り
sen-giri
julienne strips

角形の薄切りを重ねて、繊維に
添ってさらに細く切る。

Make thin cuts through a stack of
thin slabs with the grain running
in the same direction as the cut.

小口切り
koguchi-giri
edge cut

ねぎなど細長い円筒形の材料を
小口から薄く輪切り。

Starting from one end, cut long
slender cylindrical foods like
scallions crosswise thinly.

みじん切り
mijin-giri
fine chopping

せん切りをさらに小口から刻む。

Starting from one end, cut the
juliennestrips finely.

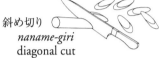

斜め切り
naname-giri
diagonal cut

細長い円筒形の材料を小口から
斜めに切る。

Starting from one end, cut long
slender cylindrical foods
diagonally.

さいの目切り
sainome-giri
cube cut

1cm角の拍子木切りをさいころ状
に切る。

Cut rectangular bars into 3/8-
inch cubes.

乱切り
ran-giri
rolling wedges

円筒形の材料を回しながら斜め
切り。

Cut cylindrical foods diagonally,
rotating.

あられ切り
arare-giri
dice cut

3～5mm角のさいころ状に切る。

Cut rectangular bars into 3/16-
inch cubes.

笹がき
sasagaki
shaving cut

ごぼうなど細い材料を鉛筆を削
るように薄くそぎながら切る。

Shave slender foods like burdock
thinly, as if sharp-ening a pencil
with a knife.

調理器具 • EQUIPMENT

泡立て器
awadateki
whisk

裏ごし器
uragoshiki
fine sieve

おろし金
oroshigane
grater

おたま
otama
ladle

落としぶた
otoshibuta
drop-lid

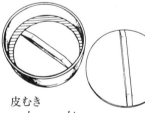

皮むき
kawamuki
peeler

缶切り
kankiri
can opener

串
kushi
skewer

計量スプーン
keiryō-supūn
measuring spoon

こし器
koshiki
strainer, colander

ざる
zaru
draining basket, sieve

しゃもじ
shamoji
flat wooden spoon

すり鉢
suribachi
grinding bowl, mortar

卵焼き鍋
tamago-yaki-nabe
square omelette pan

土鍋
do-nabe
clay pot, earthenware pot

鍋
nabe
pan, pot

箸
hashi
chopsticks

飯台
handai
wooden sushi bowl

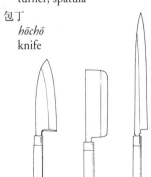

フライ返し
furaigaeshi
turner, spatula

包丁
hōchō
knife

巻き簀
makisu
bamboo rolling mat

まな板
manaita
cutting board

蒸し器
mushiki
steamer

焼き網
yakiami
cooking grill

調理用語 • COOKING TERMS

アクを取る
aku o toru
skim foam

揚げる
ageru
deep-fry

味見をする
ajimi o suru
taste

味を調える
aji o totonoeru
season

温める
atatameru
heat

油をひく
abura o hiku
grease, oil

泡立てる
awadateru
beat

いためる
itameru
sauté, stir-fry, brown

いる
iru
roast, toast

裏ごしする
uragoshi suru
strain

おろす
orosu
grate

◆

かき混ぜる
kakimazeru
stir

皮をむく
kawa o muku
peel, remove

刻む
kizamu
chop, mince

切る
kiru
cut, slice

砕く
kudaku
crumble

加える
kuwaeru
add

削る
kezuru
shave

こす
kosu
strain

こする
kosuru
rub

◆

さく
saku
tear

刺す
sasu
skewer

さます
samasu
chill, cool

さらす
sarasu
soak, rinse

絞る
shiboru
wring, squeeze

する
suru
grind

背わたを取る
sewata o toru
devein

◆

炊く
taku
cook

つける
tsukeru
dip, soak

つぶす
tsubusu
mash

溶かす
tokasu
dissolve

溶く
toku
beat

◆

煮る
niru
simmer, braise, cook, boil

塗る
nuru
brush

◆

ひく
hiku
grind

浸す
hitasu
soak

ふたをする
futa o suru
cover

沸騰させる
futtō saseru
bring to a boil

ふる
furu
sprinkle

◆

混ぜる
mazeru
toss, mix, blend, stir, combine

まぶす
mabusu
coat, dust

水けをきる
mizuke o kiru
drain

蒸す
musu
steam

◆

焼く
yaku
bake, broil, grill, roast

ゆでる
yuderu
boil, parboil

材料 • INGREDIENTS

青ねぎ
ao-negi
scallion

青のり
ao-nori
green-seaweed flakes

赤貝
aka-gai
ark shell

赤唐がらし
aka-tōgarashi
red chili pepper

あさつき
asatsuki
chive

あさり
asari
littleneck clam

あじ［魚］
aji
horse mackerel

あずき（小豆）
azuki
red beans

アスパラガス
asuparagasu
asparagus

油
abura
oil

油揚げ
aburaage
deep-fried tofu

アボカド
abokado
avocado

甘だい［魚］
amadai
red tilefish

あゆ［魚］
ayu
sweet smelt

あわび
awabi
abalone

いか
ika
cuttlefish, squid

イクラ
ikura
salmon roe

伊勢えび
ise-ebi
lobster

一味唐がらし
ichimi-tōgarashi
chili pepper flakes

いわし
iwashi
sardine

うどん
udon
wheat noodles

うなぎ
unagi
eel

うに
uni
sea urchin

梅干し
umeboshi
pickled plums

枝豆
edamame
fresh soybeans

えのきだけ
enokidake
enoki mushrooms

えび
ebi
shrimp, prawn

えんどう豆
endōmame
green peas

オクラ
okura
okra

◆

かき［貝］
kaki
oyster

柿
kaki
persimmon

片栗粉
katakuriko
cornstarch

かつお
katsuo
bonito

かつお節
katsuo-bushi
dried bonito flakes

かに
kani
crab

かぶ
kabu
turnip

かぼちゃ
kabocha
squash, pumpkin

かます［魚］
kamasu
saury pike

からし
karashi
mustard

カリフラワー
karifurawā
cauliflower

かれい［魚］
karei
flounder, halibut

寒天
kanten
agar-agar

かんぴょう
kampyō
dried gourd strips

きくらげ
kikurage
cloud ear mushrooms

きす［魚］
kisu
sillago

絹ごし豆腐
kinugoshi-dōfu
"silken" tofu

きぬさや
kinusaya
snow peas

木の芽
kinome
sansho springs

きゅうり
kyūri
cucumber

ぎんなん
ginnan
ginkgo nuts

栗
kuri
chestnuts

車えび
kuruma-ebi
shrimp

クレソン
kureson
watercress

削り節
kezuribushi
dried bonito flakes

高野豆腐
kōya-dōfu
freeze-dried tofu

小玉ねぎ
ko-tamanegi
pearl onion

ごぼう
gobō
burdock root

ごま（胡麻）
goma
sesame seeds

米
kome
rice

こんにゃく
konnyaku
devil's tongue jelly

昆布
konbu
konbu kelp

◆

さけ［魚］
sake
salmon

酒
saké
rice wine

さざえ
sazae
top shell

さつま芋
satsumaimo
sweet potato

里芋
satoimo
taro

さば［魚］
saba
mackerel

さやいんげん
saya-ingen
green beans

さやえんどう
saya-endō
snow peas

さんしょう
sanshō
prickly ash

しいたけ
shiitake
shiitake mushrooms

しし唐がらし
shishi-tōgarashi
small green pepper

しそ
shiso
shiso leaves, perilla

舌びらめ
shita-birame
sole

七味唐がらし
shichimi-tōgarashi
seven-spice pepper

しめじ
shimeji
shimeji mushrooms

じゃが芋
jagaimo
potato

春菊
shungiku
chrysanthemum leaves

しょうが
shōga
fresh ginger

しょうゆ
shōyu
soy sauce

白玉粉
shiratamako
glutinous riceflour

酢
su
vinegar

すずき［魚］
suzuki
sea bass

そうめん
sōmen
fine wheat noodles

そば
soba
buckwheat noodles

◆

たい［魚］
tai
sea bream

大根
daikon
daikon, long white radish

大豆
daizu
soybeans

竹の子
takenoko
bamboo shoots

たこ
tako
octopus

玉ねぎ
tamanegi
onion

たら
tara
cod

唐がらし
tōgarashi
chili pepper

豆腐
tōfu
bean curd

長芋
nagaimo
mountain yam

長ねぎ
naganegi
Japanese leek

なす
nasu
eggplant

なめこ
nameko
nameko mushrooms

にしん
nishin
herring

にんじん
ninjin
carrot

ねぎ
negi
Japanese leek

のり
nori
nori seaweed

◆

白菜
hakusai
Chinese cabbage

はす（蓮）
hasu
lotus root

はまぐり
hamaguri
hard-shell clam

春雨
harusame
saifun noodles

ピーマン
pīman
green pepper

ひらめ［魚］
hirame
flounder, halibut

麩（ふ）
fu
wheat gluten

ふき（蕗）
fuki
coltsfoot

ぶり［魚］
buri
yellowtail

ブロッコリー
burokkorî
broccoli

紅しょうが
beni-shōga
red pickled ginger

ほうれん草
hōensō
spinach

帆立て貝
hotate-gai
scallop

◆

まぐろ
maguro
tuna

松たけ
matsutake
matsutake mushrooms

みそ
miso
fermented soybean paste

三つ葉
mitsuba
trefoil

みりん
mirin
sweet rice wine

めばる［魚］
mebaru
rockfish

もち（餅）
mochi
glutinous rice cakes

木綿豆腐
momen-dōfu
"cotton" tofu

れんこん
renkon
lotus root

◆

山の芋
yama no imo
mountain yam

ゆず
yuzu
yuzu citron

◆

わかめ
wakame
wakame seaweed

わさび
wasabi
wasabi horseradish

素材別索引・INDEX

装幀●菊地信義
装画●野村俊夫

撮影●宮本　進
レイアウト●ポイントライン

料理製作●大阪あべの辻調理師専門学校—日本料理研究室

英語で日本料理
100 Recipes from Japanese Cooking

1997年3月10日　第1刷発行
2008年8月29日　第19刷発行

著　者　　畑耕一郎

　　　　　近藤一樹

発行者　　富田 充

発行所　　講談社インターナショナル株式会社
　　　　　〒112-8652　東京都文京区音羽1-17-14
　　　　　電話　03-3944-6493（編集部）
　　　　　　　　03-3944-6492（営業部・業務部）
　　　　　ホームページ　www.kodansha-intl.com

印刷・製本所　大日本印刷株式会社

ISBN 978-4-7700-2079-6